MW00723490

Let There Be
Light

Pastor Raymond H. Vietmeier

ISBN 978-1-0980-6071-8 (paperback)
ISBN 978-1-0980-6473-0 (hardcover)
ISBN 978-1-0980-6072-5 (digital)

Copyright © 2020 by Pastor Raymond H. Vietmeier

All rights reserved. No part of this publication may be reproduced, distributed, or transmitted in any form or by any means, including photocopying, recording, or other electronic or mechanical methods without the prior written permission of the publisher. For permission requests, solicit the publisher via the address below.

Christian Faith Publishing, Inc.
832 Park Avenue
Meadville, PA 16335
www.christianfaithpublishing.com

Printed in the United States of America

CHAPTER 1

Who Needs to See the Light?

This is probably not an unexpected chapter name for a Christian book. If you have read my first book, *The Book of Scripture vs. Culture*, you already know that there is this battle going on in the heavens, the universe, the entire world, in our own country, and in our own minds. Like I mentioned in that first book, with God's guidance, I once wrote a sermon about the battle going on inside our own minds. This battle is between good and evil. It is the battle between God and Satan. It is a battle between the righteous and the unrighteous. It is also a battle within ourselves. So based on all of these battles going on, who needs to see the light? The answer is, everyone. The details behind this statement are what this book is all about.

Before going further, I would like to point out two things about my use of italics. If an author wishes to emphasize certain words, they are not to be in all caps or underlined, or even in bold print. They are to be in *italics*. However, there are two different uses of italics when writing books. If the author wishes to emphasize words of his or her own and not quoting from the Bible, they must use italics. If on the other hand they quote scriptures, those words that are in italics are those of the author and not those of the Bible.

Now that that is clear I want to explain why everyone must strive to live in the light and also what happens when we chose via our own free will which God gave us. We do have the ability to use our free will to turn away from God and his Son, Jesus, in order to return to the dark world from which we may have come.

Yes, I personally have witnessed this myself, and some of you may have as well. I even know of a person who not only was born again with all their heart, all their soul, and all their mind but also even moved their whole immediate family to be together while the father attend a Bible college to become an ordained preacher. Then after a while, the father returned to the dark world which was obviously by his own free will. Then he committed extremely sinful actions. We hear in the news about preachers who kill their wives in order to be with their mistress. We also are finding out about preachers who have committed sexual immorality with little children. We hear about Catholic priests who have fathered babies with nuns. I know this may be a shock for many who read these words, but what I have just written are in the news reported on TV and in the newspapers.

As an ordained independent minister or nondenominational preacher, I try my best to back up everything I say in either of two ways. I am quoting either what was reported in the news or scriptures that prove every point I make. I will quote scriptures that show that even though one was once saved and was born again can turn away from God and decide to live in the dark world which is headed to and controlled by Satan and his demonic beings. The person I just told you whom I know personally who attended a Bible college laughed about it. In his own words, he told people, including myself, "I am just slip sliding away." Jesus warned us about the fact that we need to live in the light as children of light before darkness of the dark world overtakes us.

> You are going to have the light just a little while longer. Walk while you have the light, before the darkness overtakes you. Whoever walks in the dark does not know where they are going. (John 12:35)

> If you are convinced that you are a guide for the blind, a light for those who are in the dark, an

instructor of the foolish, a teacher of little children, because you have in the law the embodiment of knowledge and truth—you, then, who teaches others, do you not teach yourself? (Romans 2:19–21)

For you were once darkness, but now you are light in the Lord. Live as children of light (for the fruit of the light consists of all goodness, righteousness and truth) find out what pleases the Lord. Have nothing to do with the fruitless deeds of darkness but rather expose them. (Ephesians 5:8–11)

Knowing that this person I knew and told you about has studied the Bible and knows the scriptures just quoted, how on earth can he commit such sinful acts repeatedly with no remorse or any desire to repent? I was and still am completely baffled at that one.

These verses I just quoted teach us that we who are teachers who live in the light must also see the light as well as those who we have the God-given assignment to teach. That is, those who live in the dark world and do not know where they are going. We who live and walk in the light are not to join them, but we are to *expose them.* This is especially important for those of us who are supposed to be the teachers of those who do not know any better.

Jesus said that we must live in the light because that is the only way God can consider us his children—children who will see his kingdom. The children of light can enter heaven because upon being born again, they became one of many children of light. However, Jesus cautions the children of light about failing to be fruitful, about obeying his commands as he obeyed his Father's commands. Later I will also quote scriptures that tell us that those who turn away from God and turn to the dark world to commit specific sins including murder, idolatry, sexual immorality, slander, and swindlers "will not receive any inheritance in the kingdom of God and Jesus." I personally take that to mean they will not be allowed to enter heaven but will end up in hell. Although we cannot, as mere humans, say who will wind up in hell, we can observe those acts by certain people who the Bible says will end up in hell.

> I am the true vine, and my Father is the gardener. He cuts off each branch in me that bears no fruit, while every branch that bear fruit he prunes so that it will be even more fruitful. You are already clean because of the word I have spoken to you. Remain in me, as I also remain in you. No branch can bear fruit by itself; it must remain in the vine. *"which is Jesus"* Neither can you bear fruit unless you remain in me.
>
> I am the vine; you are the branches. If you remain in me and I in you, you will bear much fruit; apart from me you can do nothing. If you do not remain in me, you are like a branch that is thrown away and withers; such branches are picked up, thrown into the fire and burned. If you remain in me and my words remain in you, ask whatever you wish, and it will be done for you. This is to my Father's glory, that you bear much fruit, showing yourselves to be my disciples.
>
> As the Father has loved me, so have I loved you. Now remain in my love. If you keep my commands you will remain in my love, just as I have kept my Father's commands and remain in in his love. I have told you this so that my joy may be in you and that your joy may be complete. My command is this: Love each other as I have loved you. (John 15:1–12)

Those of you who have been taught that once saved always saved, please take notice what Jesus said in John 15. He said that *you must remain in him and that you must remain in his love.* That implies that somehow you are able to no longer remain in him and also no longer remain in his love even though you were once born again and were in him and he was in you. He also states that *you must obey his commands* if you want to remain in his love and remain in him and he in you.

If we who are children of light fail to be fruitful, we are warned of the repercussions of being cut from Jesus and thrown away to wither and then thrown into the fire to be burned. To be fruitful, I believe, means to grow as Christians and not simply say that because you were born again you need to do nothing else. Jesus said you must do two things in order to be fruitful and not cut away from he who is the vine. We do not want to quit being fruitful unless we wish to be thrown down to be withered and then thrown into the fire to be burned. I am not exaggerating this one bit. That means that we will no longer be in Jesus and Jesus will no longer be in us. We are cut from Jesus, the vine. Our bodies are no longer a temple in which the Holy Trinity resides. We will learn later, according to scripture, about what happens when our bodies are vacated by the Holy Trinity. I will leave that for later.

Also, we remain children of light because we grow as Christians. To grow as Christians, we become fruitful, and we also must continue to obey Jesus's commands. Additionally, we must expose all those who are in the dark according to the above quote from Ephesians.

In the second week of September 2019, I listened to the morning news on CBS. A person involved in a study of what is important in our culture today was being interviewed. He reported that the results of this study was that the young people of today's culture seem to be more concerned with themselves than the old but long-standing, admired attitude of looking out for each other. Jesus even said that there is no greater love than for one to give his life for another. Those who serve in the military and risk their lives for those they love back home and even those they don't even know back home demonstrate this much greater love.

He also stated that his study showed that having children is no longer a high priority among the youth of today. Plus, people are beginning to worry more about what the government can do for them rather than what can they do for the government. He said that according to his study, the young of today's culture are more likely to vote for the democrats in politics because they promise they will give free college and health care. However, they fail to tell us where the money will come from to accomplish all this. Just the promise is enough for today's youth.

As I listened, I could tell by his study that the days of the old Democratic Party of Pres. Harry Truman, Pres. Jimmy Carter, and Pres. John Fitzgerald Kennedy have changed. It was President Kennedy who stated, *"Ask not what your country can do for you. Ask what you can do for our country."* The candidates for public office in the new Democratic Party are now promising many things the government of our country can do for the people. They stress that there should be free college for all. Also, there should be free health care for all. They are now catering to the youth who feel everyone owes them everything, and they do not owe anything to anyone else. This is the way of a typical socialistic government. In fact, we hear in the news that some of those who call themselves democrats are actually socialists. Bernie Sanders has proudly stated that he is a socialist.

What the youth fail to understand is that once in power, the leaders of a socialist government are also more interested in themselves and what everyone in the country can do for them as well. They originally promise the world to the people. But in a socialist government, it is the leaders of the government that gets all the great benefits, and they somehow forget what they promised to the people. As I said before, they fail to say where all the money would come from in order to provide all these things for free. They say they will tax the rich heavily. However, in a socialist government, only the members of the political party are the rich. Companies are owned by the government, so there are no rich who own Ford, GM, Walmart, or other huge company. Even the news media is under government control and is considered a state-run media.

It is also easy to see this battle between good and evil going on in the world with the radicalized haters of everyone but their own. What seems to be so ironic to me is the fact that those who are radicalized think that killing anyone who is not radicalized like themselves must die because that is what God wants. We are told by those who are Muslims that the Koran does not talk about Muslims killing other Muslims. Nor does it say Muslims should kill Christians and Jews. In fact, we are told they are not to kill anyone. One of the Ten Commandments states, *"Thou shall not kill."* Another reason for my believing what the true Muslims state is that when God had my wife and I join a nondenominational church, the pastor held a study of the Koran. I know what the Koran says. It says nothing about Muslims killing anyone. It states that only God will kill.

Keep in mind that in today's world, the leaders of government of Iran finances all the various radicalized factions. There are the Hezbollah, Muslim Brotherhood, ISIS, Al-Qaida, Taliban, and others. According to a CBN News report, the backers of the government consist of only 10 percent of the Iranian population. This is according to their news report of July 12, 2019. In fact, the other 90 percent actually prefer the way of life we have in the United States. They say they love the United States. They even say they love Israel. That tells me that it is only the very small 10 percent led by the reigning Iranian government that wants to eliminate Israel from the face of the earth. This is not what the Koran teaches. Even the leaders of Iran are more interested in themselves rather than looking out for others, including their own people.

It was also reported in September 2019 by CBN News that Iran now has the fastest-growing conversion to Christianity of all nations in the world. Why should there be a sudden switch in Iran? Could it be that because Pres. Donald J. Trump called Iran out and "exposed them" as a nation of darkness when he said Iran is one of the top evil empires in the world? I will now repeat a previous quote from Ephesians 8:

> For you were once darkness, but now you are light in the Lord. Live as children of light (for the fruit of the light consists of all goodness, righteousness and truth) find out what pleases the Lord. Have nothing to do with the fruitless deeds of darkness but rather *expose them.*

Notice that while President Obama gave Iran millions of American dollars in his "Iran deal," President Trump did the opposite. He *"exposed them"* as those who are evil and live in the dark which, by the way, is headed by Satan. The dark world is Satan's domain.

As I stated in an earlier book, President Trump has a team of clergy from many different denominations meet with him each morning before any other business is conducted unless, of course, there is an immediate emergency. They pray over all the things going on in the world. He relies on God to guide him in leading the country. When God hears many people praying as a group, he pays close attention to those prayers. God is pouring out his Spirit upon the earth these days like never before. I have been on the earth for seventy-six years and have witnessed many miracles from our Father, but never have I seen the outpouring of his divine Spirit upon entire nations like he has in recent times.

For those who do not realize it, Pres. Abraham Lincoln was the first Republican president of the United States. Yes, his first name was that of Abraham just like the man whom God made into the great nation of Israel. Remember what God told Abram before he renamed him Abraham in the book of Genesis.

> The LORD had said to Abram. Go from your country, your people and your father's household to the land I will show you. I will make you a great nation, and I will bless you; I will make your name great, and you will be a blessing. I will bless those who bless you, and whoever curses you I will curse; and all peoples on earth will be blessed through you. So Abram went, as the LORD had told him; and Lot went with him. Abram was seventy-five years old when he set out from Harran. He took his wife Sarai, his nephew Lot, and the possessions they had accumulated and the people they had acquired in Harran and they set out for the land of Canaan, and they arrived there. (Genesis 12:1–5)

The leaders of Iran say they know the Bible as well as the Koran. If that is the case, why in the world would they want to eliminate Israel from the face of the earth? Did they fail to read Genesis 12? I'll tell you why. Because they live in the dark world of Satan and need to be *"exposed."* Like Jesus said, "They do not know where they are going."

Please notice in that biblical quote from Genesis that God said he would bless his name and later he changes his name to Abraham. That is the same name of our first Republican party's president, Abraham Lincoln. Now I cannot say for sure that President Lincoln was blessed because of his name. I can say that the Bible teaches us that God has a plan for each person he creates.

We have exposed other nations of being in the evil dark world. There is China and North Korea who are killing Christian pastors and burning their churches. They also burn any Bibles they find. The most troubling thing to me is what was reported during the month of September 2019. People in China and North Korea are told to spy on family members and neighbors. They are to report to the authorities anyone who has a Bible or talks about Christianity to anyone. Why? They say that in a communist nation, which is another word for *socialism*, that it is the government that becomes the god of the people. Therefore, it is against the law for the people to worship any other god, especially the one and only God Almighty who created everything and resides in heaven with his glorious Son, Jesus, at his side.

For any reader who questions if communism is the same as socialism, remember the full name of the Soviet Union: the United Soviet Socialist Republic (USSR). In the Russian alphabet, it is CCCP. Yes, they are one and the same. I strongly request you read a book that tells the truth about communism and socialism. Please read George Orwell's *Animal Farm*.

We also must *expose* those within the government of the United States of America who live in the dark. It is also easy to see the battle going on in our own government. Almost half of the population lives in the dark. They cause violent protests against President Trump. They try their best to show the people that he has done many things that are illegal. They have yet to succeed. I personally do not like those attacks, but as one of many new prophets, I feel that God has caused the opposing party to bring on those attacks. I believe it just may be that when the attacks turn out to be politically motivated and not based on the truth, the people will see the truth and vote the way God wishes them to vote. Yes, I believe God has placed President Trump in the White House in order to help get God's work done. They attack this president like no other president has ever been attacked by senators and representatives in the United States before. The only thing close was the attack against Pres. Abraham Lincoln. There was a four-year Civil War over that one.

Take Pres. John F. Kennedy for example. It was well-known that he considered the late actress Marilyn Monroe his mistress. Yet the Democrats in our government try their best to show that President Trump is a womanizer and abuser of females and call him a racist as well. It was well-known that President Clinton was a womanizer. He was impeached only because he lied to Congress about his actions.

While adultery is very strongly renounced throughout the Bible, we must remember that David, whom God declared as one of his favorite people, committed adultery. He lived with Bathsheba, the wife of another man.

We must expose those in our government who are in the dark and do not know where they are going. The majority of Democrats are now in favor of allowing abortions to those babies that are actually born or even shortly after their live birth. The states that are considered Republican are now passing laws to abolish abortions whenever a heartbeat is detected. When a human's heart stops beating and there is no brain activity, we consider them dead. When one's heart is beating; their brain is functioning; they are able to move their arms and legs, open and close their eyes, make verbal sounds, and even react to differences in noises and movement, they are considered to be alive. How then can it not be considered evil in the eyes of God to murder a baby when all these bodily functions are active and especially after full birth?

I watched a newscast on TV where two female Democratic senators said that we need to do away with our current Constitution because it no longer meets the needs of our society. Do you realize what that means? Every amendment to our Constitution—all the laws that have been passed—are all flushed down the drain. We no longer have freedom of speech, freedom of religion, freedom to bear arms, and the right to any of the rights expressed in the current Constitution. These are the same evil people who want to take "In God We Trust" off our currency. They want to remove the Ten Commandments from our courthouses. They want to stop any mention of God in our schools. Today's CBN News included the reporting of a college that banned a Christian-based organization and expelled its students who were members. The Democrats want to stop everyone from praying in public. That means that we would no longer be allowed to give thanks to God before eating in a restaurant without breaking the law. I don't know about you, but I love to see people, especially families, pray before they eat regardless if it is at home or at a restaurant. What is wrong with thanking in God who is our Creator and supplier of everything? Remember the popular reality show *Duck Dynasty*. That show was cancelled because the members of the Robertson family prayed before meals and openly expressed their Christian views. The dark world hates those who live in the light.

The atheist says that demonstrating our belief in God in public offends them. Well, don't we have the same rights as they? Is it not offensive to us who believe in our Creator and to know that those people are filing lawsuits against anything that refers to Christianity? Even the ACLU, which is a Democratic Party creation, is assisting with these lawsuits. They attack anything and everything dealing with those who believe in God. How then can a true born-again Christian, one of the children of light, stand to see this happening in our society? Furthermore, how can they back the Democratic Party platform which advocates all these evil things, all the while demonstrating hatred toward those who believe in God, our wondrous Lord and Creator?

Before continuing, I wish to acknowledge that I know I am repeating many things and quoting many scriptures that are also found in my first book, *The Book of Scripture vs. Culture*. As God is inspiring the writing of this book as well, he wants me to repeat these things for two reasons: there are those who did not read that first book and need to know some of the key issues presented therein that God wants them to know. Also, God wants me to branch off into a new direction with his teaching, and it needs to have these things repeated so that many who are children of light know the truth.

I would now like to quote from the unanimous declaration of the United States of America, which is also known as the Declaration of Independence.

> When in the course of human events, it becomes necessary for one people to dissolve the political bands which have connected them with another, and to assume among the powers of the earth, the separate and equal station to which the Laws of Nature and of Nature's God entitled them, and decent respect to the opinions of mankind requires that they should declare the causes which impel them to the separation.
>
> We hold these truths to be self-evident, that all men are created equal, that they are endowed by their Creator with certain unalienable Rights, that among these are Life, Liberty and the pursuit of Happiness. That to secure these rights, Governments are instituted among men, deriving their just powers from the consent of the governed.

Now if we declare that we should not pray whenever we choose, we are stating that the foundation of our Untied States of America was not done with the intent that the people *are endowed by their Creator with certain unalienable rights.* Does not the word *Creator* refer to our heavenly Father who created everything? In the first quote, it also states in the last few words, *"Nature's God entitled them."* That, my friends, is a very powerful statement. Anyone who tries to do away with God in this country is trying to reverse our founding fathers' intent. It is also the duty of all judges and especially the Supreme Court to uphold the words of the Constitution and the intent for the meaning of those words by our founding fathers. We are to be a nation that recognizes God. If the atheists say they are offended by the mention of God in our government, they need to find a different nation in which to live because this nation was founded *"under God."* It is the other way around. Since this country was founded under God, those who want to do away with God are offending the majority of this nation's population, not to mention our late founding fathers. That is why we have in our pledge of allegiance, *"One nation under God."*

I love to see people in public with T-shirts and hats that state, "One nation under God." Now that we have covered the evil darkness that looms within our government, it is time to expose those in our society. I probably do not have to spell it out in great detail. We know by watching the news who these evil people are. They are not only those who commit crimes but anyone who declares that God is not the Creator, that Jesus is not the Son of God, that they are offended when anyone who loves the Lord God and his only Son try to express their belief and practice their belief. They want to take away our right of freedom of religion. Well, I think what they are saying is that they have no religion, so they are free to believe as they do. That is true. Just don't try to force everyone else in the country to believe as the atheists do. If you read 1 John, you will see a similarity here. It is that the direction into which many are trying to guide us is exactly what those known as the Gnostics, the people who say they know everything, tried to guide Christians in the early Churches started by the apostle John.

No, I will not quote every verse that pertains to John's references to the false teachings of the Gnostics from 1 John. I will spare you all that reading, but I will list the things that the Gnostics did try to teach the early Christians. These are the main falsehoods the Gnostics tried to preach to the Christians.

The lack of assurance of salvation. However, John does mention that there are sins that do not result in death, but there are those that do result in death.

About the total lack of morality. John points out that "The one who does what is sinful is of the devil because the devil has been sinning from the beginning. The reason the Son of God appeared was to destroy the devil's work."

The Gnostic teaching that Jesus was not the Son of God. I would like to mention that it is written that if a spirit does *not* acknowledge that Jesus is the Son of God, that spirit is of the devil. Any Spirit that *does* acknowledge that Jesus is the Son of God that Spirit is of God.

The warning against denying the Son of God. John once points out that it is Satan who is the liar. Jesus even called Satan the father of lies. Jesus also states that Satan has been a liar and a murderer from the beginning.

The Gnostic teaching of disobedience of Christ's commands. Yes, the Gnostic believed and taught the Christians in disobedience of Christ's commands.

The false Gnostic teaching that it is okay to not love your brothers and sisters in Christ. As you well know, one of Jesus's commands is to love your brothers and sisters.

Now comes the most important part of this chapter. As the title suggests, we should know who needs to see the light. Wow! This chapter, although it seems to be full of criticisms toward the Democratic Party, it really is not. This chapter simply points out those who live in the dark, those whom the Bible tells us should be *"exposed."* It would be great if all those who we are able to identify as those living in the dark could be somehow transformed into seeing the light. That is not possible. But it is the job of the children of light to at least show those who live in the dark that living in the light won't hurt them. As children of light, we must let our light shine for those in the dark world of Satan to see.

Chapter 2 will be more informative as to what we children of light must do about the darkness we have exposed. Notice that we should not condemn those who live in the dark. They simply do not know any better. They are lost and do not know where they are going according to Jesus. However, by exposing them, we allow everyone to see who and what they really are and what they want to do to our society, our culture.

CHAPTER 2

What Does God Want the Children of Light to Do?

One thing that the children of light must do in order to grow as a Christian and become more fruitful is to strive to be more like Jesus. When we were born again, we said or implied that we would follow Jesus and strive to be more like him. If we obey Jesus's commands to "Love your enemy as yourself," "Love your neighbor as yourself," and then simply, "Love each other," then we are at least trying to be more like Jesus. Just about every Christian knows that it is also written that we are to be fast to listen but slow to speak and slow to anger. That is the way Jesus lived. If we are to follow Jesus's ways, we should practice our way of living to be as close as possible to the ways of Jesus. Remember, Jesus was very critical of the Pharisees and the money changers at the temple. However, he simply pointed out where they were going wrong. They were already living like the Romans who were people of the world which is ruled by Satan. Jesus was calling the Pharisees hypocrites.

Some Pharisees, such as Nicodemus, truly believed that Jesus came from God and was sent by God to perform miracles that only could be done through God.

We children of light can shine our wondrous light all day and night by living like Jesus so that some of those who live in the dark may see the light and change. Just like the song by Hank Williams

Jr., "I Saw the Light." However, those who are bent on staying in the dark cannot be convinced by seeing our light shine and change their ways. They enjoy their life in the dark. As Jesus told his disciples when they were sent out into the world to preach, if they do not listen to you, shake the dust off your sandals and move on. There are those who just refuse to listen or repent, and there is nothing you or I can do to help them see the light.

At this point, I wish to interject a special note. One of my assignments from God is to council people whom God sends my way. Some of these people have serious problems, emotional problems, or problems with understanding what God wants of them. I have learned that with all the many things he has assigned me to do, I am serving two purposes. Firstly, I am to try to help the person whom God sends my way. Secondly, I am also to learn from such experiences.

One such person God sent said she had severe emotional problems and was seeing a therapist. I told her that seeing a therapist may just be the answer, but if it does not help, I would always be there for her if she wanted me to offer help from a Christian viewpoint rather than a secular one. She immediately stated that she was a born-again Christian. At one point, she wanted to talk to me about seeking my help. In preparation for our first real meeting, God did not tell me what her problem was. Instead, he simply gave me a list of questions to ask her. He told me that by asking her these questions, I would be able to identify her problem.

As a result of the questions I was instructed to ask it was obvious to me that although she was a born-again Christian at one time, she decided to use her free will to turn away from God and commit one of the major sins mentioned in both 1 Corinthians and Romans. Those were the sins that would cause the person to not receive any inheritance in the kingdom of God or Jesus. You see, God does not tamper with our free will. He will, however, use his servants, like myself, to try to influence those who have drifted away from him by explaining what God has to say in his inspired words in the Bible.

When a person commits a sin that God detests, he will turn them over to their sin or lust and no longer reside in them, and their body will no longer be a temple in which he will reside. She declared several things that only would come from Satan. I could see that she was listening to either Satan or repeating things that others got from listening to Satan.

The book of Romans said that in these cases the person must both repent and stop committing the horrible sin which they have been duped into thinking is perfectly okay. There is more to the story, though. She said two things that I could feel God saw as insults. She stated that she always believed this way even though she claimed to be a true Christian. Additionally, she was trying to influence another person into committing the same sin even though the other person expressed a feeling of great guilt. That feeling of guilt is the Holy Spirit telling the person they are about to do something terribly wrong—sinful and evil. By trying to influence this person to not feel guilt, she was also trying to get her to use her free will to turn away from God. She was now guilty of the first sin, stating that God created her that way, which is untrue, and also trying to persuade another to sin. Upon explaining about her need to repent and stop committing this sin as it is stated in the book of Romans, I gave her a copy of the quotations from Romans.

When she refused to repent and stop committing her sinful acts, I asked God what I should do. He reminded me of the scripture where Jesus told his disciples that if they do not listen to my teaching, I am to simply shake the dust off my sandals and move on. It hurts me to know that there are those I cannot help. They do not want help if it means they have to repent and ask for forgiveness and then stop their sinful ways. I then realized God knew she would not repent or change her ways. Our heavenly Father wanted me to experience this firsthand so that it would be a lesson for me, his servant.

This experience reminded me of the book of Hosea. In that book, God wanted Hosea to experience what God was experiencing when his people did not reciprocate his love for them. He ordered Hosea to marry Gomer, a prostitute. He loved her, but like God's people, she did not reciprocate his love. Instead, she kept on earning money and silver as a prostitute. Then when she finally realized that she needed to change and be a good wife, she refused to continue her act with her favorite and very rich client. The client punished her by turning her over to his sons who savagely beat her, raped her, and eventually put her up for auction as a slave to anyone who would buy her. Hosea bought her because God ordered him to reconcile with his wife. He simply wanted Hosea to experience the same kind of treatment he, our Lord, was experiencing. Although I have just bent the subject slightly, it does show how God works with his prophets, and now God does consider me one of his many new prophets.

My assignment concerning this lady with the emotional problems was because God wants me to act in a chaplain-like capacity. As a prophet, I am to relay what God wants all people to know what he wants, and also as a chaplain, I can help individuals on a one-by-one basis. God told me he would send me people to whom I am to preach to in a private setting and try to help them in any way I can to know what God expects of them. This was the first of such persons.

I wondered why God gave me a list of questions instead of telling me what the person's problem was. God does work in mysterious ways. That person no longer wants to speak to me or have anything to do with me. Yes, there are those who love living in the dark even though they may have once been born-again Christians. Due to our free will which God gave us, we have the ability to turn away from God and turn to the dark word of Satan. God said in the book of Romans that he would turn them over to their lust or sin. I believe that by turning them over to their sin that God was done with them. That means that the Holy Trinity would no longer exist in that person's body and leave a void. To fill that void, Satan would send his demonic beings to take the place where the Holy Trinity had been residing. The reason I believe this is it is written that there are certain sins that result in death. It is written in both the book of Romans and in 1 Corinthians that those who are guilty of murder, theft, adultery, sexual immorality, idolatry, and swindling will not inherit the kingdom of God.

I now quote 1 Corinthians 6:9–10, "Or do you not know that wrongdoers will not inherit the kingdom of God Do not be deceived: Neither the sexually immoral nor idolaters nor adulterers nor men who have sex with men or thieves nor the greedy nor drunkards nor slanderers nor swindlers will inherit the kingdom of God."

Verses 18–20 add this: "Free from sexual immorality. All other sins a person commits are outside the body, but whoever sins sexually sins against their own body. Do you not know that your bodies are temples of the Holy Spirit, who is in you, whom you have received from God? You are not your own; you were bought at a price. Therefore honor God with your bodies."

It is also written in the book of Romans that God will accept them back if they repent and stop committing those sins just mentioned. In my trying to help this person, God wanted me to use the term that he "detests" rather than "hates" those sins. Once they repent in true sincerity, they will return to their born-again status and not lose their salvation. God will once more return to their bodies as his temple. We do have a free will, and we can use that free will to turn away from God. Hopefully, as a result of listening to a pastor, disciple, prophet, or teacher of Christianity, the person will also use their free will in reverse. They will return to God and turn away from the dark world of Satan.

I mentioned before that as a preacher who preaches directly from the Bible, I want to make something very clear to those who read these words. I mentioned a lot of important things that are in the book of Romans. So that you do not think I am making up the things I wrote earlier, I now quote from the book of Romans.

> To those who by persistence in doing good seek glory, honor and immortality, he will give eternal life. But for those who are self-seeking and who reject the truth and follow evil, there will be wrath and anger. There will be trouble and distress for every human being who does evil. (Romans 2:7–9)

Under the heading of "God's Wrath against Sinful Humanity," I quoted what the book of Romans had to say in God's inspired words.

> The wrath of God is being revealed from heaven against all the godlessness and wickedness of peo-

ple, who suppress the truth by their wickedness, since what may be known about God is plain to them, because God has made it plain to them. For since the creation of the world God's invisible qualities—his eternal power and divine nature—have been clearly seen, being understood from what has been made, so that people are without excuse.

For although they knew God, they neither glorified him as God nor gave thanks to him, but their thinking became futile and their foolish hearts were darkened. Although they lied to be wise, they because fools and exchanged the glory of the immortal God for images made to look like a mortal human being and birds and animals and reptiles.

Therefore God gave them over to the sinful desires of their hearts to sexual impurity for the degrading of their bodies with one another. They exchanged the truth about God for lies, and worshiped and served created things rather than a Creator—who is forever praised. Amen.

Because of this, God gave them over to shameful lusts. Even their women exchanged natural sexual relations for unnatural ones. In the same way the men also abandoned natural relations with women and were inflamed with lust for one another. Men committed shameful acts with other men, and received in themselves the due penalty for their error.

Furthermore, just as they did not think it worthwhile to retain the knowledge of God, so God gave them over to a depraved mind, so that they do what ought not to be done. They have become filled with every kind of wickedness, evil, greed and depravity. They are full of envy, murder, strife, deceit and malice. They are gossips, slanderers, God-haters, insolent, arrogant and boastful; they invent ways of doing evil; they disobey their parents; they have no understanding, no fidelity, no love, no mercy. Although they know God's righteous decree that those who do such things deserve death, they not only continue to do these very things but also approved of those who practice them. (Romans 1:18–32)

There are those, however, when it is brought to their attention that they are living in the dark are willing to at least listen. We are not to just stand there looking at them. We must study the Bible in order to know what we can say to them to help them see the light and leave the dark.

Each of us who is a born-again child of God has a duty to perform. We have an obligation to find out what God wants us to do for him. We are to find out what pleases our Lord. I am thankful that in the case study mentioned above that God gave me directions by telling me what questions I should ask the person presented before me. God knew that as an ordained preacher who has written many sermons that my Bible studies would lead me to the correct conclusion as to what this person's real problem is. I figured it out, but God told me anyway that this person now has demonic beings occupying the place in their body where the Holy Trinity had been. The person refused to change and thought that instead of quoting the Bible I was using my own thoughts. She told me, "You cannot help but use your own thoughts because it comes from your self-conscience."

Because of my *spiritual gift* of discernment, I could tell that these words were given to her from Satan. She also told me that sexual immorality is not that bad of sin because it is only representing 1 percent of the Bible. That again sounds like something Satan would tell a person. If a person lives in the dark, they are listening to what Satan has to say and ignoring God; they turned away from God and no longer try to find out what pleases him.

Satan is the one who tells people that the words in the Bible were written by man and they are not God's inspired words. Yet in the book of Acts, we learn that the Holy Spirit descended upon the disciples and gave them the same powers that Jesus had while he was on earth. Many who commit those most severe sins say that it is okay for them to do what they are doing because even though it says not to in the Bible, the words were not those of Jesus himself. So that makes their sinful actions acceptable. Plus we see the culture of our society leaning in that same direction—the direction of leaving God and joining Satan in his dark world.

I knew right away that it was Satan that this person was listening to. God would never make those kinds of statements. Those who have a close relationship with God know that all the words written in the Bible are his own inspired words. Only Satan would accuse the words in the Bible as being from man, and not from God. The person also stated that they have been like that forever. When that statement was made, God made me feel that he was insulted. If a person is committing a sin and claims that they were always that way, then they are saying that God created them that way. That is not only an insult to God but is totally illogical. Why would God create a person to be a sinner of sins that result in death right from the beginning? He would not create a person to commit a sin that is one of those of which God despises so adamantly. He despises those sins so much that he is willing to turn that person over to their sin and leave their body and no longer consider it his temple.

You need to know that our Father in heaven has issued different types of service to him. In addition to acting in a chaplain-like capacity for those whom God sends to me, I am to act as a prophet and write Christian books to let the world know what he wants and expects of us. That is exactly what the prophets of the Old Testament were assigned to do. They wrote what God wanted the people to know, and it just so happens that those writings became books of the Bible.

Additionally, I am to continue my hobby of painting landscapes, but from now on, it must have a scripture-based theme. I also am to continue writing new Christian songs for him and produce a second CD to give to people free of charge.

He gave me lessons that even I did not know were lessons until later in life. I noticed that God often assigns the most important assignments when the person becomes elderly. This was the case with Moses building the ark and writing the first five books of the Bible. This was also the case with Abram (Abraham) and his wife, Sari (Sarah). Sometimes, God appoints some people to do his work by first letting them look back and see how he guided and trained them so that they may become more equipped to do his work. Then there are those assignments that must be accomplished for the person to grow as a Christian and bear much fruit. That assignment is to become a disciple and preach the Gospel to others so that they might be saved from eternal damnation. If a true Christian refuses to preach about Jesus to others and that person ends up in hell instead of being saved, it is partially the fault of the Christian who did nothing.

Each of you who is a born-again Christian, a child of light, God's child, must study and read the Bible regularly in order to keep learning. The Bible is no small pamphlet. It is a book of instructions from God and a tool to be used as a guide. Through our Bible studies, we learn what God expects of us. I want to stress that once one becomes born again, it is not the end of their duty to God. They must grow and become fruitful by obtaining wisdom and knowledge. Not everyone can attend a Bible college. Not everyone is expected to be a biblical scholar. Each of you are expected to gain wisdom and knowledge in what the heavenly Father wants you to know and to know how to conduct yourself in a world which is guided by Satan and filled with people who hate both you and Jesus. Even in the Old Testament, the book of Proverbs tells us that we are to seek wisdom and knowledge and store the wisdom in our hearts. God looks for wisdom in the hearts of both the righteous and unrighteous according to the book of Proverbs. I cannot quote all of the book of proverbs that pertain to the seeking and storing of wisdom. I encouraged you to read that book as part of your Bible study sessions.

There are those who profess to not even believe in God, Jesus, or any religion. To them, it is "Do as you wish, and nothing will happen except you will enjoy your life looking out for number one." With that statement, they obviously are thinking only of themselves and have no intent on trying to learn what God expects of them. They are in the dark world and love every minute they spend in it. They listen to the lies of Satan and believe every word he tells them.

When a person commits a sin such as murder, theft, sexual immorality, idolatry, or swindling, God considers them to be committing the evilest of sins. Therefore, God will no longer allow them to enter his kingdom. They will not be accepted into heaven.

Paul wrote his first letter to the Church of Corinth, "I have the right to do anything," you say—but not everything is beneficial. "I have the right to do anything"—but I will not be mastered by anything. You say, 'Food for the stomach and the stomach for food, and God will destroy them both.' The body, however, is not meant for sexual immorality but for the Lord, and the Lord for the body" (1 Corinthians 6:12–13).

You must know that one thing expected of the children of light is to completely give their body to God the Father. It is as though you get down on your knees and say to God, "Here I am, Lord. Do as you please with me. I am completely committed to your will."

I will not lie to you or mislead you. That statement made in the previous paragraph was first made my Gordon Robertson, the son of Pat Robertson of CBN, one of my favorite networks. In fact, there are times when I am interrupted by God to stop what I am doing and to turn on CBN, DayStar, or other Christian programming because there is something being said to which I should pay attention. I love working for God. He is absolutely amazing and wonderful.

It is the will of God that children of light obey Jesus's commands—all of Jesus' commands. That includes showing love and having love in your heart and soul for everyone. There will be some that all you can do is pray that somehow God will send his Spirit to convince them to come to him and be one of us. While that would be nice, I firmly believe God intended the children of light to try to convince the nonbelievers and the ones who follow the dark world's way of life to change their minds and turn to God and follow his son, Jesus.

We must try our best to get those people to use their free will in reverse of how they had previously used their free will. Originally, they were with God the Father, God the Son, and God the Holy

Spirit—the Holy Trinity. Then they used there free will to turn away from God and listen to what Satan was telling them. We must try to get them to use their free will once more and turn away from the dark and return to God by repenting and leaving their sinful ways. One thing that Jesus often said in the Bible was, "Sin no more." However, when the *New International Version* (NIV) Bible was written as the result of biblical experts retranslating the original languages, they realized that Jesus was actually saying, "Leave your sinful ways." I suspect that that latter term was not something common in the old English language as written in the *King James Version* (KJV).

We can also pray for those who hold elected and appointed government offices, especially those who are bent on not wanting to change their anti-God ways. In that case, we have the power to vote them out of office. Anyone who professes to kill babies at or shortly after the time of birth, and even before the time of their birth, does not deserve to hold an office in the Senate, House of Representatives, or any office at any level in the United States. Anyone who wants to do away with the government as it was set up under God does not deserve to hold any such offices. However, we must first pray for them to change. Then if they refuse to change, we simply vote them out of office. We need our country to remain as it was intended to be, a God-loving country. Even the Supreme Court makes their decisions based on the Constitution.

As one of many new prophets, I have been instructed by God to do something else. In addition to getting his words out to the people to let them know what he expects of them, he also wants the new prophets to know what the consequences of failing to do what he wishes. That is, God is divulging what will happen in the future through his prophets. God told me that if we are not successful in changing the current direction of our culture in the United States, God will no longer bless this nation. That is extremely urgent, my friends. You may not want to believe what I say, but please believe what God expects. He expects us to pattern our culture as it obey his commands and instructions found in the Holy Bible.

"Blessed is the nation whose God is the Lord, the people he chose for his inheritance" (Psalm 33:12).

When you read that quote, you can tell that the opposite is also true. You see, if God blesses those nations that acknowledge him as their Lord God and the people will get his inheritance, then those nations that do not acknowledge him as their Lord God will inherit nothing. Not only does this concern the government, but all who live in this country should know what the founding fathers intended our country to be, especially the Supreme Court, which is to make their decisions solely based on which argument before them best agrees with the Constitution. Unfortunately, our Supreme Court has begun to make decisions based on what our current culture is dictating and not what the Constitution says. Why then are some senators openly stating that we need to do away with our current Constitution because it no longer meets the needs of our culture? This is completely wrong. If that happens, we will be officially headed down a path that will cause the United States to no longer be blessed by God, and we will become a third world country. This is very serious business. The life of every person in this country depends on the path we take.

Therefore, all children of light must band together and fight by voting into office greater numbers for those who seek government offices. We need to vote for those who will go strictly by the Constitution and not our failing culture.

CHAPTER 3

Warning: Do Not Turn Away from God

Christians who study the Bible and attend services in order to grow as Christians and to become more fruitful know some of what I am about to write. Yet many who are good righteous Christians are not aware of some things. I will now present these things so that everyone who reads this book is presented with the truth about these things. What are these things we must know?

I want to bring to light those scriptures that tell us how we are in danger of not living in the Sprit. When we live in the Spirit, we also are close to our Father in heaven. We can feel that closeness. I'm talking about a special closeness that is with us constantly and not only when we pray. We must train ourselves to store this living in the Spirit in our hearts. One of the things we learn from scriptures is that Satan studies each one of us. He hates humans because we were created by God. Satan hates God and everything he creates. When he is able to get a person to fall for his evil trickery, he delights in torturing that person. When he gets them to tell a lie, he has them put a flaw in the lie. This is not to hurt the person being lied to but to hurt the person who tells the lie. He loves to destroy our lives.

How does he manage to do this, you may ask? Satan studies each one of us so that he knows each person's weaknesses and desires. He then holds out a carrot, to use a common phrase, that caters to our weaknesses and/or our desires. Then we go for the carrot and fall into his pit of trickery.

I will begin by quoting from the book of Proverbs for two reasons: first, to show how Satan tricks us into falling for his trickery based on our desires; second, the need for us to seek wisdom and store it in our hearts. Most of the book of Proverbs tells us how to avoid being tricked into doing evil and living a life of unrighteousness.

> The righteousness of the blameless makes their paths straight, but the wicked are brought down by their own wickedness. The righteousness of the upright delivers them, but the unfaithful are trapped by evil desires. (Proverbs 11:5–6)

> My son, if sinful men entice you, do not give in to them. If they say. "Come along with us: let's lie in wait for innocent blood, let's ambush some harmless soul; let's swallow them alive, like the grave, and whole, like those who go down to the pit; we will get all sorts of valuable things and fill our houses with plunder; cast lots with us; we will all share the loot"—my son, do not go along with them, do not set foot on their paths; for their feet rush into evil, they are swift to shed blood. How useless to spread a net where every bird can see it! These men lie in wait for their own blood; the ambush only themselves! Such are the paths of all who go after ill-gotten gain; it takes away the life of those who get it. (Proverbs 1:10–19)

If we examine the above quote, we find that many of the things that are mentioned do not involve every one of us. However, we see gangs advocating such actions, and they get a righteous person to do evil in order to be accepted by the gang as one of their own. Solomon was teaching his son how to avoid falling for the evil trickery that comes from Satan to get us to do his will and not that of our Creator, our heavenly Father.

The next quote from Proverbs tells us the moral benefits of wisdom.

> My son, if you accept my words and store up my commands within you, turning your ear to wisdom and applying your heart to understanding—indeed, if you call out for insight and cry aloud for understanding, and if you look for it as for silver and search for it as for hidden treasure, then you will understand the fear of the LORD and find the knowledge of God. For the LORD gives wisdom; from his mouth come knowledge and understanding. He holds success in store for the upright, he is a shield to those whose walk is blameless, for he guards the course of the just and protects the way of his faithful ones. Then you will understand what is right and just and fair—every good path. For wisdom will enter your heart, and knowledge will be pleasant to your soul. Discretion will protect you, and understanding will guard you. Wisdom will save you from the ways of wicked men, from men whose words are perverse, who have left the straight paths to walk in dark ways, who delight in doing wrong and rejoice in the perverseness of evil, whose paths are crooked and who are devious in their ways. (Proverbs 2:1–15)

In chapter 3, we learn how wisdom bestows well-being.

> My son, do not forget my teaching but keep my commands in your heart, for they will prolong your life many years and bring you peace and prosperity. Let love and faithfulness never leave

you; bind them around your neck, write then on the tablet of your heart. Then you will win favor and a good name in the sight of God and man. Trust in the LORD with all your heart and lean not on your own understanding; in all your ways submit to him, and he will make your paths straight. Do not be wise in your own eyes; fear the LORD and shun evil. This will bring health to your body and nourishment to your bones. Honor the LORD with your wealth, with first-fruits of all your crops; then your barns will be filled to overflowing, and your vats will brim over with new wine. (Proverbs 3:1–10)

Chapter 4 tells us that we should get wisdom at any cost.

I give you sound learning, so do not forsake my teaching. For I too was a son to my father, still tender, and cherished by my mother. Then he taught me, and he said to me, "take hold of my words with all your heart; keep my commands, and you will live. Get wisdom, get understanding; do not forget my words or turn away from them. Do not forsake wisdom, and she will protect you; love her, and she will watch over you. The beginning of wisdom is this: Get wisdom. Though it cost all you have, get understanding. Cherish her, and she will exalt you; embrace her, and she will honor you. She will give you a garland to grace your head and present you with a glorious crown." Listen, my son, accept what I say, and the years of your life will be many. I instruct you in the way of wisdom and lead you along straight paths. When you walk, your steps will not be hampered; when you run, you will not stumble. Hold on to instruction, do not let it go; guard it well, for it is your life. Do not set foot on the path of the wicked or walk in the way of evildoers. Avoid it, do not travel on it; turn from it and go on your way. For they cannot rest until they do evil; they are robbed of sleep till they make someone stumble. (Proverbs 4:2–16)

We also learn from other scriptures how we must conduct ourselves in order to avoid leading a sinful life, a life of evilness.

Therefore, do not let sin reign in your mortal body so that you obey its evil desires. Do not offer any part of yourself to sin as an instrument of wickedness, but rather offer yourselves to God as those who have been brought from death to life; and offer every part of yourself to him as an instrument of righteousness. (Romans 6:12–13)

Therefore do not let sin reign in our mortal body so that you obey its evil desires. (Romans 6:12)

As it is, it is no longer I myself who do it, but it is sin living in me. For I know that good itself does not swell in me, that is, in my sinful nature. For I have the desire to do what is good, but I cannot carry it out. For I do not do the good I want to do, but the evil I do not want to do—this I keep on doing. Now if I do what I do not want to do, it is no longer I who do it, but it is sin living in me that does it. (Romans 7:17–20)

Therefore, I urge you, brothers and sisters, in view of God's mercy, to offer your bodies as a living sacrifice, holy and pleasing to God—this is your true and proper worship. Do not conform to the pattern of this world, but be transformed

by the renewing of your mind. Then you will be
able to test and approve what God's will is—his
good, pleasing and perfect will. (Romans 12:1–2)

In the book of Galatians, we find that we must walk in the
Spirit. Earlier I said that when we walk in the Spirit, we have a certain
closeness with our Creator.

So I say, walk by the Spirit and you will not gratify the desires of the flesh, For the flesh desires
what is contrary to the Spirit, and the Spirit what
is contrary to the flesh. They are in conflict with
each other, so that you are not to do whatever
you want. But if you are led by the Spirit, you are
not under the law.

The acts of the flesh are obvious: sexual
immorality, impurity and debauchery; idolatry
and witchcraft; hatred, discord, jealousy, fits of
rage, selfish ambition, dissensions, factions and
envy, drunkenness, orgies, and the like. I warn
you, as I did before, that those who live like this
will not inherit the kingdom of God. (Galatians
5:16–20)

No one who is born of God will continue to sin,
because God's seed remains in them; they cannot go on sinning, because they have been born
of God. This is how we know who the children
of God are and who the children of the devil
are: anyone who does not do what is right is not
God's child, nor is anyone who does not love
their brother and sister. (1 John 3:9–10)

CHAPTER 4

Dealing with the Ignorance of Our Immigrants and Voting Youth

I listened to a reporter on television interviewing young people of voting age recently. One question was, "When was the United States Constitution signed?"

The person seemed confused at first but then came up with their answer, "I believe it was in 2006." Similar questions which should have been taught in our schools were asked, and answers that were just as stupid showing a total lack of knowledge were frequent. Only a very small minority of those questioned knew the correct answers. I shuddered to think that these same people will be voting in our elections. If we are worried about the Russians and other countries interfering in our election, we should also be equally, if not more, concerned with those who vote and have no idea what is going on in our country.

Some could not answer who the current attorney general was. Some could not name our first president. Some could not name the three branches of our government. One person even said, "I didn't know we had branches of our government."

I know it sounds crazy, but the people who legally enter this country must be tested on such matters. If they fail the test, they will not be allowed to become citizens. The Democratic Party platform wants those illegal immigrants to be allowed to vote as well.

That makes no sense at all. It is completely political. If they can convince the illegal immigrants that they will get special treatment if they vote for Democrats, then they have succeeded in winning offices by cheating.

Likewise, should we make our students who reach voting age take the same test as those who are our newest legal citizens? If we allow illegal immigrants to vote, should they also be required to take that same test? Those who dropped out of school even before high school have no idea what our government is about. I asked one person some time ago where the state of Missouri was. He was attending high school in a city in the state of Missouri. He did not know there was a state of Missouri. I know that sounds almost unbelievable, but it is the truth. Yet they will be allowed to vote for our very important offices at the federal, state, and local levels of government.

There is one more very important issue related to our voting public. Our schools and colleges are pressing hard to advocate socialism. You may have heard on television or read in the newspapers that President Obama wrote in one of his books that he especially admired those professors who advocate communism.

There is a nonprofit conservative student organization that tries to get their views at least considered. Those college students who express any conservative viewpoint are ridiculed and emotionally abused by professors. The professors make fun of them in front of the other students in the class. If conservative students state their views to other students, they are sometimes physically abused and beaten. This must stop. Our colleges are trying to do away with our freedom of speech unless the speech is about liberalism, socialism, and communism.

The Bible tells us that we Christians will be persecuted. Jesus said in the book of John,

> If the world hates you, keep in mind that it hated
> me first, If you belonged to the world, it would
> love you as its own. As it is, you do not belong to
> the world, but I have chosen you out of the world,
> That is why the world hates you. Remember

what I told you: A servant is not greater than his
master. If they persecuted me, they will persecute
you also. If they obey my teaching they will obey
yours also. They will treat you this way because of
my name, for they do not know the one who sent
me. (John 15:18–21)

Yes, in our colleges and schools, Christians are being persecuted.
Many teachers and professors are not Christians and do not know
the one who sent Jesus; God sent Jesus to be the perfect lamb, the
lamb of God. In some schools in our country if a student states anything about God, Jesus, or the Bible, they are persecuted before their
peers. I thank God for the schools in what is commonly referred to as
the Bible Belt. In the schools of the Bible Belt, they even have Bring-
Your-Bible-to-School Day. Some school districts are now teaching
out of the Bible but often not as the true answer but as a comparison
to other views. While that is not the best way, it is at least getting
God's words heard by young students.

Although this is probably the shortest chapter in this book, it
also covers one of the most important issues ever experienced in the
United States. If we are to maintain a level of literacy in this country,
then we need to cause all illegal immigrant voters to either be tested
or deported. It may be just as important to make new voters take the
same test.

CHAPTER 5

It Is Your Primary Responsibility to Become a Disciple

Becoming one of the million "children of light" is the beginning of a life filled with a close relationship with the Holy Trinity—God the Father, God the Son, and God the Holy Spirit. It also is the way to walk in the Spirit with God and pleasing God. I will not assume that you are already born again, but I would like to explain it for you just in case you are not a born-again Christian or you are not sure you are a born-again Christian. To be born again, you also become one of God's children, children of light.

The book of John explains this in detail in a conversation between Jesus and a member of the Pharisees named Nicodemus, who was a ruler of the Jews. I would like to quote the biblical record here so you are completely familiar with the true meaning of being born again. Again, I preach from the Bible only. I must not preach of things I thought of myself but rather only the inspired words of God the Father, who is the Creator of everything.

Here is the conversation between Jesus and Nicodemus, as quoted in the book of John.

> Now there was a Pharisee, a man named Nicodemus who was a member of the Jewish ruling council. He came to Jesus at night and said,

"Rabbi, we know that you are a teacher who has come from God. For no one could perform the signs you are doing if God were not with him."

Jesus replied. "Very truly I tell you, no one can see the kingdom of God unless they are born again."

"How can someone be born when they are old?" Nicodemus asked. "Surely they cannot enter a second time into their mother's womb to be born."

Jesus answered, "Very truly I tell you, no one can enter the kingdom of God unless they are born of water and the Spirit. Flesh gives birth to flesh, but the Spirit gives birth to spirit. You should not be surprised at my saying, 'You must be born again.' The wind blows wherever it pleases. You hear its sound, but you cannot tell where it comes from or where it is going. So, it is with everyone born of the Spirit."

"How can this be?" Nicodemus asked.

"You are Israel's teacher," said Jesus, "and do you not understand these things? Very truly I tell you we speak of what we know, and we testify to what we have seen, but still you people do not accept our testimony. I have spoken to you of earthly things and you do not believe; how then will you believe if I speak of heavenly things? No one has ever gone into heaven except the one who came from heaven—the Son of Man. Just as Moses lifted up the snake in the wilderness, so the Son of Man must be lifted up, that everyone who believes may have eternal life in him."

Every true Christian lives by the very popular biblical quote in John 3:16: "For God so loved the world that he gave his one and only Son, that whoever believes in him shall not parish but have eternal life." However, it continues with these words, "For God did not send his Son into the world to condemn the world, but to save the world through him. Whoever believes in him is not condemned, but whoever does not believe stands condemned already because they have not believed in the name of God's one and only Son" (John 3:17–18).

To be born again, you must say with your mouth before others, with all your heart, all your soul, and all your mind what is commonly called a sinner's prayer.

I now quote Romans 10:8–10, "But what does it say? The word is near you; it is in your mouth and in your heart,' that is, the message concerning faith that we proclaim: If you declare with your mouth, 'Jesus is Lord,' and believe in your heart that God raised him from the dead, you will be saved. For it is with your heart that you believe and are justified, and it is with your mouth that you profess your faith and are saved."

While there is no specific wording as to what a sinner's prayer must contain, these three major things should be in the prayer: (1) a confession that you are a sinner and asking for God's forgiveness, (2) belief that Jesus is God's only Son, and (3) following Jesus and accepting him as your personal Lord and Savior.

The reason the Bible mentions the phrase "with all your heart, all your soul, and all your mind" is that only when this happens do you show God you are truly sincere without any question or reservation. Upon stating a sinner's prayer, you are then born again. Now in the book of John, Jesus said that to be born again, you must be born of both water (as in baptism) and the Spirit. Upon being born again, you now have the Holy Trinity in you, and you are in them as well.

In John 17, we read Jesus's own words as he prays his last prayer just before he is arrested. He first prays for God to glorify him, as read in John 17:1–5. Then he asks for his disciples to be joined with them so that they will be in the Holy Trinity and the Holy Trinity will be in them, as said in verses 6 through 19. Finally, in verses 20 through 26, Jesus prays for those who God has given him, those who are born again, and those who are considered God's own children of light. He prays,

> My prayer is not for then alone [meaning his disciples]. I pray also for those who will believe in me through their *message*, that all of them may be one, Father, just as you are in me and I am in you. May they also be in us so that the world may believe that you have sent me. I have given them the glory that you gave me, that they may be one as we are one—I in them and you in me—so that they may be brought to complete unity. Then the world will know that you sent me and have loved them even as you have loved me.
>
> Father, I want those you have given me to be with me where I am, and to see my glory, the glory you have given me because you loved me before the creation of the world.
>
> Righteous Father, though the world does not know you I know you, and they know that you have sent me. I have made you known to them, and will continue to make you known in order that the love you have for me may be in them and that I myself may be in them.

Remember the quote of Jesus earlier in John 12:15–36, "You are going to have the light just a little while longer. Walk while you have the light, before darkness overtakes you. Whoever walks in the dark does not know where they are going. Believe in the light while you have the light, so that you may become children of light."

That is what born-again Christians are supposed to do. We are not to stop at the prayer that allows us to become born again. Once we are born again, we are to walk in the light and turn away from the dark and find out what pleases the Lord.

In the quote earlier in Ephesians, we read the words about the fruitful deed of the dark world. What are the fruitful deeds of the dark world? To begin with, practicing such things as witchcraft, having your fortune told, playing with the outjie board, and disobeying any of God's rules and those of his Son, Jesus. Remember the most sinful of sins mentioned earlier are murder, theft, idolatry, sexual immorality, and swindling.

Paul also wrote the book of Ephesians about bearing fruit. He wrote that it was those who live in the dark that are fruitless. The children of light bear fruit because they consist of goodness, righteousness, and truth. They are to find out what pleases the Lord. They are also to turn away from the dark world and expose any of their dark and fruitless deeds.

John 15:1–15 goes much further. It is this quoting of Jesus that tells what will happen if we fail to bear fruit. God will cut us away from the vine (*Jesus*), and we will no longer be the ones whom Jesus referred to when he asked God to give to him in his final prayer before he was arrested.

Our newest generation is completely different from those in the past. The main reason the parents in the 1800s had many children is it was the children who helped their parents. If they lived in the towns and cities, they helped their parents with whatever business they had. If they lived in the country or on a farm, they had to help with the work that needed to be done. In Jesus's time, it was the same way. Jesus helped his earthly father, Joseph, in his carpentry business. He learned the valuable lessons of helping and taking care of the tools used in work. When those of us who were a child between the 1940s through 1960s, we had responsibilities. We had chores to do. We had to obey our parents, helping them and respecting them.

My parents' home was next door to a small farm which belonged to the Franciscan sisters. Along with the other boys in the neighborhood, we would help the sisters and their hired workmen throughout the year to harvest the hay and alfalfa, lift the seventy-five-pound bales onto the wagon, and then hoist the bales into the loft as feed for their cows. I'm not saying we were saints, but we knew it was the right thing to do. In the middle of the summer, it was in the low hundreds and much too hot for the nuns to do that work in their long black habits. We did not do it in order to receive glory. In fact, we did not expect any reward for helping. The nuns did give us some leftover Easter candies. They were stale and not too flavorful, but we thanked them and meant it. I mentioned in other books how I had a very close relationship with the Holy Trinity. Doing work for the nuns was simply one way of showing God our appreciation for all the things he does for us all year long.

When Jesus is in your life in a very powerful way, you look forward to helping and do not see the good deeds as a way of getting into heaven. We already knew we would be going to heaven, but we felt we should continue to bear fruit by helping others when we can.

In the Boy Scouts, it is taught that we are to do our duty to God and our country. We are to help those who have difficulty doing things themselves either because of old age or due to disabilities. When my grandmother suffered a severe stroke, my cousins and I felt honored to help her up the stairs when she came to visit us in our respective homes. We didn't complain. I have no idea how some of our youth today feels everybody owes them. Even if they do leave home and get a job, they show up late for work and think it is perfectly okay to do so. If the boss gets upset, they quit the job. They do not want to work or participate in anything that requires them to help. They like to spend their time playing games on various electronic devices.

Could it be that the parents are at fault by not making them do chores when they were younger? By reading and studying the Bible, God teaches us how to live. That includes how parents are to raise their children. It teaches the children how to show respect for their parents and do what is right and what is expected of them. If the family no longer attends church and no longer has a regular family Bible-reading session, they no longer learn what the Bible teaches.

Did the parents not attend church as a family and learn the things God wants them to know? Did the children and their parents become part of the dark world which is led by Satan?

Only God knows all the reasons so many of today's population refuse to recognize him and his wonderful Son, Jesus. I personally, along with many other pastors, believe it is our schools that are partially to blame. Schools are told not to allow the mention of Jesus,

God, or anything resembling a religion in the classroom. They cannot say a prayer at sports events. They cannot say grace before eating lunch.

The teachers are pounding the socialistic views into our children's heads. They come out of high school already aiming in the wrong direction. They teach them to take a direction that we should not maintain the old type of society which preaches goodness, righteousness, and all that is the truth. Those who go on to college are now bombarded with communistic views. Those students who listened to their parents, attend college with a righteous mind, and lean toward the conservative views are looked down upon by their socialistic peers and even violently abused.

I'm personally beginning to believe that attending a Christian college prepares the students to be of value to society. That also means they become more valuable to themselves.

The next chapter deals with what we are to do as Christians in a more specific manner. If we fail to do what is right according to the Bible, then we fail as Christians—the children of light.

CHAPTER 6

What Can Children of Light Do to Protect Our Children and Country?

In the earlier chapters, we read how everything around us seems to be turning to the dark world. Remember, Jesus said that those who live in the dark world do not know where they are going. As children of light, we are also to turn away from the dark world and *expose any of their dark and fruitless deeds*. Among other things, this chapter will address finding out who these people of the dark world are in today's society. We will read scriptures to learn what the Bible has to say about how to find out who they are. We can only do two things. We can pray for them, and we can expose them.

Earlier, we explored the various possibilities as to what is going wrong to cause the current problems with our society. I intentionally did not address what we can do about it then. I decided it would be better to look into that in this chapter.

When you look at a serious problem and wonder how things got so bad, you can only look no further than one place. Ask yourself the questions that follow:

Whom did Jesus call the father of lies and all that is false?

Whom did Jesus call a murderer from the beginning and all that is evil?

Who is the unrighteous being that decided he was better than God?

Who turned away from God and took a third of the angels with him?

Who has the knowledge and power with the help of his demons to cause all sorts of turmoil in the world which he guides?

Who has the power to turn the majority of a political party into ones who advocate killing babies unborn and now even shortly after birth? To them, unborn and even newly born babies are considered nothing.

Who has the power to cause college professors to teach those who would become teachers of our children to turn away from God?

Who is it that would have the power to turn whole families against each other and their children?

Who has the power to cause parents whether single or married to no longer attend church?

Who has the power to turning the clergy into sinners so that those who would be interested in joining a church decide to not do so because they feel churches must be just as evil as the outside world?

Who has the power to make members of the clergy of all Christian denominations into child molesters and able to commit adultery and even murder?

The answer to all eleven of these questions is Satan! The hymn written by Martin Luther, "What a Mighty Fortress Is Our God," has a powerful statement about how Satan is a powerful foe. That is so true. Here are verses 1 and 3 of this powerful hymn:

> A mighty fortress is our God. A bulwark never
> failing.
> Our helper he amid the flood of mortal ills
> prevailing.
> For still our ancient foe, doth seek to work his
> woe—
> His craft and pow'r are great, and, armed with
> cruel hate, on earth is not his equal. (Verse 1)

And tho this world, with devils filled, should
   threaten to be undoing.
We will not fear, for God hath willed his truth to
   triumph thru us.
The prince of darkness grim, we tremble not for
   him his rage we can endure.
For lo, his doom is sure. One little word shall fell
   him. (Verse 3)

Once we are able to determine who is the cause of our social
problems, we need to find out what the Christian Bible says about
how to identify those who listen to Satan and obey his commands.
They live in the dark world with Satan and belong to him. If we are
able to identify them, then we can combat this onslaught of evil. As
I mentioned earlier, the Bible tells us we are to "expose them." Since
we are to compare all things to scripture, let us read those scriptures
that tell us how we can identify those who follow the orders of the
evil one.

There is no doubt that we live among those who live in the
world of evil. The Bible tells us this. The righteous who are of God
must live in the same world as those who are of Satan. The question
we must now address is who is of God and who is of Satan, the evil
one. In 1 John, we find the answers to this very question. The reason
for turning to the scriptures is, as you will read later, John tells us to
"compare all things to scripture."

I feel that those of us who are of God, and not of Satan, need to
find out who lives as part of the dark world. Then we need to figure
out what we should do about our society's situation. What can we do
when those who are of Satan try to overcome we who are saved? We
can fight those who are not righteous and practice evil deeds because
they listen to the evil one and do exactly what he tells them to do.

There is a problem with simply trying to attack those who are
part of the dark world. Many are good people who are on the edge
of the fence and may be persuaded to change and come on our
side. If we are too bold in our attempt to fix things, we just may
scare those people away rather than getting them to turn away from

the dark world. Later we can begin to identify the hard-core lovers of the dark world and who are on the fence and may be likely to change if told the truth in a kind and gentle way. First, let us turn to scripture to see what we need to know. In the following scriptures, I have included only those passages which deal with the subject at hand. Therefore, I will skip over those parts that address a different subject.

We need to begin in 1 John at the point where John explains "Light and Darkness, Sin and Forgiveness."

Now that I have explained what to expect when we read 1 John, it is time to actually read what John has to say.

> This is the message we have heard from him and declare to you: God is light; in him there is no darkness at all. If we claim to have fellowship with him and yet walk in the darkness, we lie and do not live out the truth. But if we walk in the light, as he is in the light, we have fellowship with one another, and the blood of Jesus his Son, purifies us from all sin. If we claim to be without sin, we deceive ourselves and the truth is not in us. If we confess our sins, he is faithful and just and will forgive us our sins and purify us from all unrighteousness. If we claim we have not sinned, we make him out to be a liar and his word is not in us. (1 John 1:5–10)

> Anyone who claims to be in the light but hates a brother or sister is still in the darkness. Anyone who loves their brother and sister lives in the light, and there is nothing in them to make them stumble. But anyone who hates a brother or sister is in the darkness and walks around in the darkness. They do not know where they are going, because the darkness has blinded them. (1 John 2:10–11)

Next, John explains his reason for writing to us believers to assure us of the certainty of our faith. He wants to assure us that they can tell who is of God and who is of the evil one.

> I am writing to you dear children, because your sins have been forgiven on account of his name. I am writing to you, fathers because you know him who is from the beginning. I am writing to you, young men because you have overcome the evil one. I write to you, dear children because you know the Father. I write to you, fathers, because you know him who is from the beginning. I write to you, young men because you are strong, and the word of God lives in you, and you have overcome the evil one. Do not love the world or anything in the world. If anyone loves the world, love for the Father is not in them. For everything in the world—the lust of the flesh, the lust of the eyes, and the pride of life—comes not from the Father but from the world. The world and its desires pass away but whoever does the will of God lives forever. (1 John 2:12–14)

Next, John gave a warning against denying God's Son, Jesus.

> Dear children, this is the last hour; and as you have heard that the antichrist is coming, even now many antichrists have come. This is how we know it is the last hour. They went out from us, but they did not really belong to us, for if they had belonged to us, they would have remained with us; but their going showed that none of them belonged to us.
>
> But you have an anointing from the Holy One, and all of you know the truth. I did not write to you because you do know it and because no lie

comes from the truth. Who is the liar? It is whoever denies that Jesus is the Christ. Such a person
is the antichrist—denying the father and the Son.
No one who denies the Son has the Father; whoever acknowledges the Son has the Father also. As
for you, see that what you have heard from the
beginning remains in you. If it does, you also will
remain in the Son and in the Father. And this is
what promised us—eternal life.

I am writing these things to you about those
who are trying to lead us astray. As for you, the
anointing you received from him remains in you,
and you do not need anyone to teach you. But
as his anointing teaches you about all things and
as the anointing is real, not counterfeit—just as
it has taught you, remain in him. And now, dear
children, continue in him, so that when he appears
we may be confident and unashamed before him
at his coming. If you know that he is righteous,
you know that everyone who does what is right
has been born of him. (John 2:18–28)

We now skip to chapter 3 in 1 John, where John explains about
being led astray.

Dear children, do not let anyone lead you astray.
The one who does what is sinful is of the devil
because the devil has been sinning from the
Beginning. The reason the Son of God appeared
was to destroy the devil's work. No one who is
born of God will continue to sin, because God's
seed remains in them; they cannot go on sinning,
because they have been born of God. This is how
we know who the children of God are and who
the children of the devil are: Anyone who does
not do what is right is not God's child, nor is

anyone who does not love their brother and sister. For this is the message you heard from the beginning: We should love one another. Do not be like Cain, who belonged to the evil one and murdered his brother. And why did he murder him? Because his own actions were evil, and his brothers were righteous. Do not be surprised, my brothers and sisters, if the world hates you. We know that we have passed from death to life, because we love each other. Anyone who does not love remains in death. Anyone who hates a brother or sister is a murderer, and you know that no murderer has eternal life residing in him.

This is how we know what love is: Jesus Christ laid down his life for us. And we ought to lay down our lives for our brothers and sisters. If anyone has material possessions and sees a brother or sister in need but has no pity on them, how can the love of God be in the person? (1 John 3:7–24)

We now skip to verses 21–23.

Dear friends, if our hearts do not condemn us, we have confidence before God and receive from him anything we ask, because we keep his commands and do what pleases him. And this is his command: to believe in the name of his Son, Jesus Christ, and to love one another as he commanded us. The one who keeps God's commands lives in him, and he in them. And this is how we know that he lives in us: We know it by the Spirit he gave us. (1 John 3:21–23)

John 4 warns us about believing every spirit. It would appear to me that many good people listen to the wrong people or the wrong spirits. Just like the cartoons where an angel sits on a person's shoulder and on the opposite shoulder sits the devil. Both are trying to tell us to believe what they are saying. How then do we know which one is telling the truth?

> Dear friends, do not believe every spirit, but test the spirits to see whether they are from God, because many false prophets have gone out into the world. This is how you can recognize the Spirit of God: Every spirit that acknowledges that Jesus Christ has come in the flesh is from God, but every spirit that does not acknowledge Jesus is not from God. This is the spirit of the antichrist, which you have heard is coming and even now is already in the world. You, dear children, are from God and have overcome them. Because the one who is in you is greater than the one who is in the world. They are from the world and therefore speak from the viewpoint of the world, and the world listens to them. We are from God, and whoever knows God listens to us; but whoever is not from God does not listen to us. This is how we recognize the Spirit of truth and the spirit of falsehood. (1 John 4:1–13)

In John 5 teaches us an important lesson about whom we should trust.

> Everyone who believes that Jesus is the Christ is born of God, and everyone who loves the father loves his child as well. This is how we know that we love the children of God; by loving God and carrying out his commands. In fact, this is love for God; to keep his commands. And his commands are not burdensome, for everyone born of God overcomes the world. This is the victory

that has overcome the world, even our faith.
Who is it that overcomes the world? Only the
one who believes that Jesus is the Son of God. (1
John 5:1–5)

I believe I have covered the primary scriptures we should read to
compare what is going on in our world today. But simply identifying
those who are of the evil one and live in the dark world should not be
forgotten. In order for us to try to rebuild a better society for the sake
of ourselves and our children and our children's children, we should
try to win back those who are in the world but may be persuaded to
turn away from the dark and come to the light. I know that Jesus
said that those in the dark world hate us, but if we approach them in
a kind manner, we just may be able to convince them to come and
join us. Remember, there are some who may be in the dark world but
do not necessarily believe all of the evil things the dark world teaches
and stands for. They may be in the dark world only because they were
never told the truth. They must be told the Gospel. Remember, we
are to try to build more disciples because it is the duty of all disciples
to talk to those in the dark world and teach them the truth. If even
some will listen, more may join with them, and we can win over
enough of those people that we can improve our society and have
more people on our side. They can be persuaded to not only join us
but join us in full by being born again and be in the Father and the
Father in them. The verses I just quoted tell us how to identify those
in the dark world. However, not all who are in the dark world are
committed to staying there. The evangelist Billy Graham was successful in getting millions of the people who live in the dark world to
come and join us in the light.

The answer lies in Jesus's own words as quoted in Ephesians 5.

For you were once darkness, but now you are
light in the Lord. Live as children of light (for the
truth of the light consists in all goodness, righteousness and truth) and find out what pleases
the Lord. Have nothing to do with the fruit-

less deeds of darkness, but rather expose them.
(Ephesians 5:8–11)

That, my friends, tells us that Jesus knows that we came from the dark world. We did not all automatically become children of light by being born in the light. We came from the dark and then decided because of our free will to turn away from the dark and become children of light. I now ask that you recall the case in which God had me council someone he sent to me. That person came from the dark world, and although going through the sincere praying to be born again, that person decided with the free will which is given by God to return to the dark world. Therefore, that person could not have been that way all their life. Either that, or the person was not sincere in heart, soul, and mind upon praying to be born again. Therefore, what I am trying to say to all of you, readers, who are living in the light as children of light you should not be satisfied with just being children of light. You must become a disciple. You must try to help those who are in the dark world to see the light as you see the light. Like in the song written by Hank Williams "I Saw the Light." The words in the first verse are powerful and prove that those in the dark world can become children of light, like many of us. Here is the first verse of the Hank Williams's song.

I wondered so aimless, life filled with sin, I wouldn't let my dear savior in.
Then Jesus came like a stranger in the night, Praise the Lord, I saw the light.

Other disciples who work diligently are those in our prisons, turning those who were once evil and lived a life filled with sin into children of light. We have missionaries around the world working hard and living in places that are filled with sickness and hunger to help those who were once living in the dark to join those of us who live in the light as children of light.

When Iran financed the terrorists of so many different radicalized organizations, it did so in order to instill fear into the population so that they would fear for their lives and decide to become radicalized as well. After all, we know that those organizations decapitate Christians if they do not convert to the radical version of the Muslim religion. They wanted to cause everyone in the United States of America to become one of their own. Most of us have stood fast and did not allow them to scare us into becoming radicalized. However, there are a few within our own country who have allowed themselves to become radicalized. If you remember, President Obama and Hillary Clinton both refused to use the term "radicalized Islamic terrorists." Why? Could it be that they could not recognize the evil ones who were not born of God? Why then could they not see or recognize those who were evil and call them by what they really are? I do not wish to get political, but when certain leaders of our own country are obviously not able to recognize those who are the liars and instead are bent on rebuking those who are telling the truth, something very wrong is happening with them. We cannot allow those people to be in power in our oval office: Senate; House of Representatives; the Supreme Court; and even the law enforcement agencies like FBI, CIA, DEA, and others. It is my firm belief that the evil one, Satan, is trying his best to cause our country which was founded under God to turn to the dark world. Remember once again in the pledge of allegiance, the phrase "One Nation under God." It was some of those same leaders in the congressional branch along with the atheists who wanted to take that part out because in their minds, it violated the constitution of separation of church and state. Believe me, the atheists admit that they are not of God because they do not even believe in God or any part of any religion and especially not Christianity. Therefore, these political parties must not join in with the atheists and try to turn our entire country into a country that is opposed to God and act willingly against God.

I am old enough to remember the presidential election in 1960. So many people in the United States were concerned about John Fitzgerald Kennedy because he was a Catholic. They were concerned that his religious beliefs would influence his decisions if he were elected. He was able to maintain an equal balance between his personal beliefs and the decisions required by the office of the president of the United States.

I had the honor to serve in the navy with JFK being as the commander-in-chief of the armed forces. I was impressed when he stood up to the evil going on in Cuba. He called for the naval blockade. Now our current president, Pres. Donald Trump, is doing the same thing. He is standing up to evil all over the world. He, like JFK, is not afraid to use military force to keep those who would destroy us from succeeding. He also is not afraid to use the proper term for the evil terrorists of "radicalized Islamists."

There is one main difference, though. As I mentioned in the beginning of this book, President Trump holds a prayer meeting first thing each morning. He is guided by the Christian values that were present when this country was founded. President Lincoln used to pray throughout the day when he felt he needed guidance from our Father in heaven.

While guidance from those around us may be sufficient in some cases, you never really know the beliefs of those you support. They may say they are on your side. They may say they are of God. However, they very well may be like a wolf in sheep's clothing. They are there to lead you astray. By reading what we just did in 1 John, we found the answers as to who is trying to lead us astray. We must support those who we can be sure of being on the side of right and good instead of wrong and evil.

I said we can pray for those who are responsible for doing evil deeds or expose them. We can actually do both at the same time. I also sincerely believe there is a third thing we can do. We can become disciples. That is what we are supposed to be according to the Bible. Therefore, how to become disciples is the question at this point.

CHAPTER 7

Supporting Scriptures on "Once Saved, Always Saved"

This was touched upon earlier but only lightly. There is this very important debate among Christian denominations which should be addressed so that those who decide to become a disciple will know all of the truth. They are the ones who need to be armed not only with more than the part of the popular scriptures that tell the story of Jesus. These scriptures are called the Gospel. Again, the word *Gospel* means the "good news." In the story of the birth of Jesus, you may recall that Gabriel, the archangel sent by God, made all the important announcements to all primary parties.

Gabriel announced to Mary that she would become pregnant as the result of the Holy Spirit. Then he informed Joseph of the truth so he would marry Mary. He also announced to the shepherds in the fields watching over their flocks not to be afraid, for he is there to bring *"good news and great tidings."* He told the shepherds about the birth of Jesus and that he could be found lying in a manger wrapped in swaddling clothes. The importance of this announcement is the key words of *"good news."* That is the Gospel. Many still think the word *gospel* meant the truth. Although it is the truth, it actually means "good news."

The books of the Bible that address the life of Jesus tell all of the facts from Jesus's birth through his ultimate Crucifixion. Then they tell about how he rose from the dead on the third day and even appeared before his disciples to prove that he was going back to be with his Father in heaven, the one who sent him as a sacrifice to pay for the sins of any and all who will believe in him.

Like many times in the past, God awakened me one night at 11:00 p.m. to insert something here that is extremely important. You see, the disciple John was not convinced that Jesus was the Son of God at first. As events unfolded, he later saw the truth and soon became what many believe is the closest one of the twelve to Jesus. Just before Jesus died on the cross, he called down to Mary and said, "Mother, this is your son." And to John, his closest disciple, he said, "This is your mother." Upon Jesus's death on the cross, John took in Mary as his mother and cared for her for the rest of her life.

It should also be noted that the disciples took on the role of becoming the first evangelistic preachers. Billy Graham was the most popular evangelistic preacher of our modern times. He was able to bring in those who were not aware of who Jesus was and convince them to be born again by the thousands at most events in which he preached the gospel.

As I was working on this book, I listened to a Southern Baptist preacher who explained how in the middle of his preaching he suddenly felt the need to burst out, "We are going to build a thousand churches this year." I do believe that he and many others felt it was God speaking through him because God is very busy pouring out his Holy Spirit during these current troubled times.

I now understand why God has directed me to write books with the help of his divine guidance. When I completed chapter 3 of the original book number two, I was suddenly stopped with the realization that I did not know how to begin chapter 4. I prayed and prayed for several days asking God what he wants me to explain in the next chapter.

Then God guided me to listen to a Church of Christ preacher talk about the subject as to whether or not one can lose their salvation. The title of the sermon was "Once Saved Always Saved?" Notice that it ended in a question mark. At the end of that sermon, the preacher gave the mailing address and web address in order to receive a copy of that sermon.

I felt compelled to jot down the address to order a copy of this sermon. Because it was Sunday of the Memorial Day weekend, I would have to wait until Tuesday to put the letter in the mail requesting a copy of that sermon. God finally answered my urgent prayers. Yes, I was put on hold because the preacher who just gave that sermon quoted many very important scriptures that answered the question at hand about losing one's salvation. I had been preaching for a long time using a few scriptures that addressed this subject, but God wanted me to add those additional scriptures in this book. These additional scriptures are in the letters written to the young Christian churches. They were the final words inspired by God on the subject of salvation.

What are now presented are all the scriptures which tell the whole truth and settle the argument once and for all. Not everyone, including myself, was aware of the vast number of scriptures that reference the facts about salvation unless they have studied it thoroughly. Those denominations which teach "once saved always saved" must not have explored all the scriptures. They do not have the urge to disprove what they have been teaching for many, many years. I do not know for sure, but it seems like the denominational headquarters dictate to their churches which way they should teach about one's salvation. This is another reason I am content to be an ordained independent minister.

These scriptures are presented now because new disciples must know the whole truth so when they tell people about the Gospel they get all of the facts included. I have always relied on John 15:1–13 as the main scripture about this subject. I quoted that scripture earlier about Jesus being the vine and we are the branches. God cuts those branches away from the vine which is Jesus and casts them down to wither and die then thrown into the fire.

I now quote another scripture that deals with one's salvation. It is written that one may turn away from God to the point of having their hearts hardened and ultimately no longer love God. They no longer place God above all other things. God will deliver his wrath against those who are willfully sinful and refuse to repent or turn away from the evil darkness and thereby refuse to return to God.

Where there is an emptiness in the hearts and souls of those who once were children of light, the evil one will feel he is invited to fill that emptiness.

Here is a scripture that deals with God's wrath against sinful humanity.

> The wrath of God is being revealed from heaven against all the godlessness and wickedness of people, who suppress the truth by their wickedness, since what may be known about God is plain to them, because God has made it plain to them. For since the creation of the world God's invisible qualities—his eternal power and divine nature—have been clearly seen being understood from what has been made, so that people are without excuse.
>
> For although they knew God, they neither glorified him as God nor gave thanks to him, but their thinking became futile and their foolish hearts were darkened. Although they claimed to be wise, they became fools and exchanged the glory of the immortal God for images made to look like a mortal human being and birds and animals and reptiles.
>
> Therefore, God gave them over in the sinful desires of their hearts to sexual impurity for the degrading of their bodies with one another. They exchanged the truth about God for a lie and worshiped and served created things rather than the Creator—who is forever praised. Amen. (Romans 1:18–32)

I know I already quoted this scripture before, but I believe that God wanted it repeated because of its great importance in the argument about whether one's salvation can be lost. That scripture explains that because of one's sinful action and their refusal to leave their sinful ways, God gave them over to shameful lusts. Then I quoted Romans earlier that God despises such extremely evil acts as murder, adultery, theft, idolatry, and sexual immorality. Those who are guilty of these and refuse to repent and ask God to forgive them and take them back as well as quit committing those sins God will punish them with death.

> I am talking to you Gentiles. Inasmuch as I am the apostle to Gentiles, I take pride in my ministry in the hope that I may somehow arouse my own people (the Jews) to envy and save some of them. For if their rejection brought reconciliation to the world, what will their acceptance be but life from the dead? If the part of the dough offered as firstfruits is holy, then the whole batch is holy; if the root is holy, so are the branches.
>
> If some of the branches have been broken off, and you, though a wild olive shoot, have been grafted in among the others and now share in the nourishing sap from the olive root, do not consider yourself to be superior to those other branches. If you do, consider this: You do not support the root, but the root supports you. You will say then, 'Branches were broken off so that I could be grafted in.' Granted. But they were broken off because of unbelief, and you stand by faith. Do not be arrogant, but tremble. For if God did not spare the natural branches, he will not spare you either.
>
> Consider therefore the kindness and sternness of God; sternness to those who fell, but kindness to you, provided that you continue in his kindness. Otherwise, you also will be cut off. And if they do not persist in unbelief, they will be grafted in, for God is able to graft them in again. After all, if you were cut out of an olive tree that is wild by

nature, and contrary to nature were grafted into the cultivated olive tree, how much more readily will these, the natural branches be grafted into their own olive tree! (Romans 11:13–21)

Now under the heading of instructions for Christian living, we turn to Ephesians 4:18.

They are hardened in their understanding and separated from the life of God because of the ignorance that is in them due to the hardening of their hearts. (Ephesians 4:18)

In Hebrews 3, there is a warning against unbelief.

See to it, brothers and sisters, that none of you has a sinful, unbelieving heart that turns away from the living God. But encourage one another daily, as long as it is called "Today," so that none of you may be hardened by sin's deceitfulness. (Hebrews 3:12–13)

And now here is another scripture dealing with salvation or the loss of.

Those who live according to the flesh have their minds set on what the flesh desires; but those who live in accordance with the Spirit have their minds set on what the Spirit desires. The mind governed by the flesh is death, but the mind governed by the Spirit is life and peace. The mind governed by the flesh is hostile to God; it does not submit to God's law, nor can it do so. Those who are in the realm of the flesh cannot please God.

You, however, are not in the realm of the flesh but are in the realm of the Spirit, if indeed the Spirit of God lives in you, And if anyone does not have the Spirit of Christ, they do not belong to Christ. But if Christ is in you, then even though your body is subject to death because of sin, the Spirit gives life because of righteousness. And if the Spirit of him who raised Jesus from the dead is living in you, he who raised Christ from the dead will also give life to your mortal bodies because of his Spirit who lives in you.

Therefore, brothers and sisters, we have an obligation—but it is not to the flesh, to live according to it. For if you live according to the flesh, you will die; but if by the Spirit you put to death the misdeeds of the body, you will live. For those who are led by the Spirits of God are the children of God. The Spirit you received does not make you slaves, so that you live in fear again; rather, the Spirit you received brought about your adoption to sonship. And by him we cry, "Abba, Father." (Romans 8:5–1)

In Galatians 5:22, we find even more truth about turning away from God and his Son, Jesus. However, it is important to include the whole story. Therefore, let us begin with verse 13. This is under the heading of life by the Spirit.

You, my brothers and sisters were called to be free *(meaning free will)*. But do not use your freedom to indulge the flesh; rather, serve one another humbly in love. For the entire law is fulfilled in keeping this one command: "Love your neighbor as yourself." If you bite and devour each other, watch out or you will be destroyed by each other. So I say, walk by the Spirit, and you will not gratify the desires of the flesh. For the flesh desires what is contrary to the Spirit, and the Spirit what is contrary to the flesh. They are in conflict with each other, so that you are not to do whatever you want. But if you are led by the Spirit, you are not under the law.

The acts of the flesh are obvious; sexual immorality, impurity and debauchery; idolatry and witchcraft, hatred, discord, jealousy, fits of rage, selfish ambition, dissensions, factions and envy; drunkenness, orgies, and the like. I warn you, as I did before, that those who live like this will not inherit the kingdom of God. But the fruit of the Spirit is love, joy, peace, forbearance, kindness, goodness, faithfulness, gentleness and self-control. Against such things there is no law. Those who belong to Christ Jesus have crucified the flesh with its passions and desires. Since we live by the Spirit, let us keep in step with the Spirit. Let us not become conceited, provoking and envying each other. (Galatians 5:22)

Please notice the extremely important words about the fact that those who are guilty of such sin *will not inherit the kingdom of God.* That means they will not go to heaven. There is only one other place they can be sent to upon their death here on this earth—hell! Now we who are brothers and sisters in Christ cannot say who will go to heaven and who will go to hell. That is something that only our wonderful Creator can decide. However, since the words just quoted are the inspired words of the Creator, it can be taken seriously as the truth. God cannot lie. Neither can his inspired words lie.

CHAPTER 8

The Things New Christians
Must Learn to Live As
Children of Light

This next chapter is intended for the new Christians. The reason God wanted me to include these scriptures is because Satan loves to pick on new Christians with his trickery. He knows that because they are new Christians and have not had the opportunity to learn the basic things every Christian should strive to learn that they are more gullible and can be persuaded more easily. To that, I would like to add that new pastors and new lay persons in any church are also seen by Satan as being easier to trick. Even Eve, the wife God made for Adam, was new in the creation of God, and Satan snuck right in and began to trick her. She fell for it and then caused her husband, Adam, to join her in her sin.

Therefore, it is of the utmost importance that new Christians, new church leaders, and those who want to grow as a Christian and become more fruitful should be aware that Satan will try to pick on you. Therefore, God wanted this chapter named "The Things New Christians Must Learn to Live As Children of Light" to include the following scriptures. These are very important scriptures of which everyone should be aware. So for those of you who have been a Christian for a long time, it may pay to at least read these scriptures to make sure you know those scriptures that God considers required reading by all Christians.

Let us now begin with the many lessons of Jesus which we all should learn in order to remain children of light. We will begin with those lessons Jesus taught and are quoted in Matthew 5.

> Now when Jesus saw the crowds, he went up on a mountainside (the Sermon on the Mount) and sat down. His disciples came to Jesus, and he began to teach them in the Sermon on the Mount.
>
> The Beatitudes:
>
> He said:
>
> Blessed are the poor in spirit, for theirs is the kingdom of heaven.
>
> Blessed are those who morn, for they will be comforted. (Also see Isaiah 61:2–3.)
>
> Blessed are the meek, for they will inherit the earth. (Also see Psalm 17:11.)
>
> Blessed are those who hunger and thirst for righteousness, for they will be filled. (Also see Isaiah 55:1–2.)
>
> Blessed are the merciful, for they will be shown mercy.
>
> Blessed are the pure in heart, for they will see God. (Also see Hebrews 12:14.)
>
> Blessed are the peacemakers, for they will be called children of God. (Also see Romans 14:19 and Isaiah 3:18.)
>
> Blessed are those who are persecuted because of righteousness, for theirs is the kingdom of heaven. (Also see Matthew 25:34.) (Matthew 5:3–10)

Then the King will say to those on his right,
'Come, you who are blessed by my Father; take
your inheritance, the kingdom prepared for you
since the creation of the world. (Matthew 25:34)

Blessed are you when people insult you, persecute you and falsely say all kinds of evil against
you because of me. Rejoice and be glad, because
great is your reward in heaven, for in the same
way they persecuted the prophets who were
before you. (Matthew 5:11–12)

You are the salt of the earth. But if the salt loses
its saltiness, how can it be made salty again? It is
no longer good for anything, except to be thrown
out and trampled underfoot.

    You are the light of the world. A town built
on a hill cannot be hidden. Neither do people light
a lamp and put it under a bowl. Instead they put
it on its stand, and it gives light to everyone in the
house. In the same way, let your light shine before
others, that they may see your good deeds and glorify your Father in heaven. (Matthew 5:13–16)

Jesus now teaches about the fulfillment of the law in verses 17
through 20:

Do not think that I have come to abolish the
Law or the Prophets; I have not come to abolish them but to fulfill them. For truly I tell you,
until heaven and earth disappear, not the smallest
letter, not the least stroke of a pen, will by any
means disappear from the Law until everything
is accomplished. Therefore anyone who sets aside
one of the least of these commands and teaches
others accordingly will be called least in the

kingdom of heaven, but whoever practices and teaches these commands will be called great in the kingdom of heaven. For I tell you that unless your righteousness surpasses that of the Pharisees and the teachers of the law, you will certainly not enter the kingdom of heaven. (Matthew 5:17–20)

Jesus addresses murder:

You have heard that it was said to the people long ago, "You shall not murder, and anyone who murders will be subject to judgment." But I tell you that anyone who is angry with a brother or sister will be subject to judgement. Again, anyone who says to a brother or sister, "Raca," (from the Aramaic term for empty-headed) is answerable to the court. And anyone who says. "You fool!" will be in danger of the fire of hell. Therefore, if you are offering your gift at the altar and there remember that your brother or sister has something against you, leave your gift there in front of the alter. First go and be reconciled to them; then come and offer your gift.

Settle matters quickly with your adversary who is taking you to court. Do it while you are still together on the way, or your adversary may hand you over to the judge, and the judge may hand you over to the officer, and you may be thrown into prison. Truly I tell you, you will not get out until you have paid the last penny. (Matthew 5:21–26)

Next, Jesus addresses adultery:

You have heard that it was said, "You shall not commit adultery." But I tell you that anyone who looks at a woman lustfully has already committed adultery with her in his heart. If your right eye causes you to stumble, gouge it out and throw it away. It is better for you to lose one part of your body than for your whole body to be thrown into hell. And if your right hand causes you to stumble, cut it off and throw it away. It is better for you to lose one part of your body than for your whole body to go into hell. (Matthew 27–30)

Now it is taught by most denominations that Jesus is not talking literally about cutting any part of the body off. Instead, it is believed he is stressing the importance of not committing adultery. In the book of Proverbs, the lessons Solomon is teaching his sons repeat the importance of staying away from those who would cause you to commit adultery, especially those women who love to get married men to commit adultery.

When I preach about the book of Proverbs, I like to tell the congregation that God gave us the Ten Commandments in order to tell us all the things we must not do. But because God loves details, it is my personal opinion that God inspired Solomon to write detailed lessons as to how not commit the sins of the Ten Commandments.

Jesus addresses divorce:

It has been said, "Anyone who divorces his wife must give her a certificate of divorce." But I tell you that anyone who divorces his wife, except for sexual immorality, makes her a victim of adultery, and anyone who marries a divorced woman commits adultery. (Matthew 5:31–32)

The taking of oaths is addressed next:

Again, you have heard that it was said to the people long ago, "Do not break your oath, but fulfill to the Lord the vows you have made." But I tell you, do not swear an oath at all: either by heaven, for it is God's throne; or by the earth, for it is his footstool;

> or by Jerusalem, for it is the city of the Great King.
> And do not swear by your head, for you cannot
> make even one hair white or black. All you need to
> say is simply "Yes" or "No"; anything beyond this
> comes from the evil one. (Matthew 5:33–37)

I now change the subject to bring you readers to the importance God puts on his chosen people, the Jews. In that last scripture,
we read that Jesus said Jerusalem is the city of the Great King. In
Geneses 12, we learned that God would make Abram (Abraham)
into a great nation and that anyone who blesses him God will bless as
well. However, God said that anyone who curses him, he, God, will
curse. Therefore, there is no question about the importance of Israel
to God. Those in our government who make derogatory remarks
about the Jews or criticize President Trump for moving the American
embassy from Tel Aviv to the biblical capital of Israel, which is
Jerusalem. Those who do this should be aware that God will curse
them as he promised in Geneses 12. This, I believe, is one lesson all
new Christians should learn and hold tight in their heart and mind.

I would also like to add that I sincerely believe what John taught
us about being born again. He stressed that to be born again, you will
have to say with your mouth before others that you confess to God
that you are a sinner, asking for his forgiveness, acknowledging that
Jesus is the only Son of God, and want to follow Jesus and accept
him as your personal Lord and Savior. I see this as a *vow* to God and
is not meant to be an oath per say. This is a vow before God that you
commit yourself with all your heart, all your soul, and all your mind.
It is the same as the vows you say at your wedding are vows to God
and not an oath. However, it is most important that you keep these
vows unless you wish to be seen as a liar before God.

Elsewhere in Matthew 19, Jesus is responding to questioning
about divorce with the Pharisees.

> Some Pharisees came to him to test him. They
> asked, "Is it lawful for a man to divorce his wife
> for any and every reason?"

"Haven't you read," he replied, "that at the beginning the Creator 'made them male and female,' and said. 'For this reason a man will leave his father and mother and be united to his wife, and the two will become one flesh'? So they are no longer two, but one flesh. Therefore what God has joined together, let no one separate."

"Why then," they asked, "did Moses command that a man give his wife a certificate of divorce and send her away?"

Jesus replied, "Moses permitted you to divorce your wives because your hearts were hard. But it was not this way from the beginning. I tell you that anyone who divorces his wife, except for sexual immorality, and marries another woman commits adultery."

"The disciples said to him, if this is the situation between a husband and wife, it is better not to marry."

Jesus replied. "Not everyone can accept this word, but only those to whom it has been given. For there are eunuchs who were born that way, and there are eunuchs by others—and there are those who choose to live like eunuchs for the sake of the kingdom of heaven. The one who can accept this should accept it." (Matthew 19:3–12)

I bring you to the use of the word *eunuchs*. It is not a common word. According to my Bible dictionary, it came from the Greek word *eulegein*, which means "guardian of the bed, a castrated man."

In 1 Corinthians, we find Paul explaining about when a married man or woman is concerned with things of the world. Also, he talks about how to please their spouse.

Unmarried men and women are concerned with the affairs of the Lord. They give undivided

> devotion to the Lord. I now introduce the fact that Moses allowed for divorce if a spouse refuses to become a believer or has hardened their heart. If a man or woman marries an atheist or someone of another religion and then tries to convert him/her to Christianity and is not successful they are permitted to file for divorce using the terms under Moses' law. The one who has a hardened heart is not going to submit to the teachings of Jesus. (1 Corinthians 7:32–35)

Therefore, my late wife and I have made it very clear to both our children that when they are serious about looking for a spouse, they should try to find someone who was raised as a true Christian like they were or is at least willing to becoming a Christian. We told them it saves a lot of trouble if they look for someone who was raised much like themselves.

In our culture today, too many people decide to live together outside of marriage and use that experience to see if they feel that the next step should be marriage. The Bible teaches us that we must not live in sin. We must not have sexual relations outside of marriage; but as sinners, as we all are, sometimes we slip up and have sex outside of marriage. We should not continue to do so without any remorse or repentance before God. It is most damaging to any child who is born of a couple who are not married because there is no vow to stay together, "For better or for worse, for richer or for poorer, in sickness or in health, until death do us part." They simply go in separate directions, and the children usually end up with a single mother without a divorce that requires the father to provide financially for the children he fathered. This adds to the poverty because a mother must now try to figure out a way to raise her children and work as well. That requires paying for child day care most of the time, unless a family member is able to provide day care.

Anyone who has children knows that it is not an inexpensive situation. How can she care for her children, earn money by working, and feed her fatherless family all by herself?

Marriage is most important. Without marriage, there is no way for a fatherless family to stay out of poverty unless the mother is sufficiently rich. In many cases, this adds to the crime rate. The children grow up angry and must resort to crime in order to stay alive. The song by Elvis Presley "In the Ghetto" explains this situation very vividly. There was a situation in the early days of our country when pioneers out west had no church or preacher to marry them. This was the beginning of what is known as the "common-law marriage." A man and wife become officially married after eight years of living together as a couple. Now it is possible to have a civil marriage by a justice of the peace or judge or a Christian marriage in a church or a marriage performed by other religions standards.

Concerning the taking of oaths, there are denominations that consider the oath of allegiance such as that of the United States of America to be against their belief. Their members are told not to take such an oath. Some denominations also see the oath one takes upon joining the armed forces so they teach their members not to take such an oath. There is also the oath an immigrant takes upon becoming a citizen of the United States. I will not quote the entire scripture, but it is in Matthew 5:33–37.

I will pass by the "eye for an eye" quotes in Matthew because it is often too confusing for the new Christian. This book is intended to explain the teachings of Jesus on how to be children of light, also referred to as one of God's people.

About love for our enemies: This is one of Jesus greatest commands which we must obey in order to stay in him and him in us. I now quote Jesus's words in Matthew about this command.

> You have heard that is was said, "Love your neighbor and hate your enemy." But I tell you, love your enemies and pray for those who persecute you, that you may be children of your Father in heaven. He causes his sun to rise on the evil and the good, and sends rain on the righteous and the unrighteous. If you love those who love you, what reward will you get? Are not even the

tax collectors doing that? And if you greet only your own people, what are you doing more than others? Do not even pagans do that? Be perfect, therefore, as your heavenly Father is perfect. (Matthew 5:43–48)

About giving to the needy, I quote Jesus's teaching in Matthew.

Be careful not to practice your righteousness in front of others to be seen by them. If you do, you will have no reward from your Father in heaven.

So when you give to the needy, do not announce it with trumpets, as the hypocrites do in the synagogues and on the streets, to be honored by others. Truly I tell you, they have received their reward in full. But when you give to the needy, do not let your left hand know what your right hand is doing, so that your giving may be in secret. Then your Father, who sees what is done in secret, will reward you. (Matthew 6:1–4)

About prayer, I quote Jesus from Matthew 6:5–15.

And when you pray, do not be like the hypocrites, for they love to pray standing in the synagogues and on the street corners to be seen by others. Truly I tell you, they have received their reward in full. But when you pray, go into your room, close the door and pray to your Father, who is unseen. Then your Father, who sees what is done in secret, will reward you. And when you pray, do not keep on babbling like pagans, for they think they will be heard because of their many words. Do not be like them, for your Father knows what you need before you ask him.

I would like to interject something here about God knowing what you need without you even asking. This was mentioned in my first book.

When my ordained son and I were preaching in a nursing home, a situation arose. My son called one Saturday night all excited because he got a message from God as to what the topic of tomorrow's sermon should be. He knew the topic well and was ready to give the service.

Sunday morning, I awoke feeling very ill. I knew it was Satan trying to keep me from going to the church service. Having serious health problems myself and since my son had everything under control, I would just rest. But God gave me a message, "Get ready to go to the nursing home. Mike needs you urgently." I only hesitated for a few seconds when the message was repeated with a little more enthusiasm. "Get ready to go to the nursing home. Mike needs you urgently!"

Not wanting to disobey God, I hurried to the nursing home. There I played hymns on the piano while the congregation filed in. At exactly 10:00 a.m., when the service was to begin, my cell phone rang. It was my son, Mike. "Dad, my wife is having a very serious diabetic attack, and I can't leave her alone. Can you please handle the service today?"

I assured him I would. I began with the opening pastoral prayer, and with my head still bowed, I realized that I had not prepared a sermon, and my son did not tell me what topic God wanted him to use in today's sermon. In order to not look unprepared to the congregation, I began to pray with my head still bowed. Like the quote of Jesus just given, "Do not be like them, for your Father knows what you need before you ask him." Yes, God knew exactly what I was going to pray for and gave me the topic of today's sermon even before I could finish the prayer. As it turns out, it was the same topic God sent in his message to my son the night before.

I now continue the quote from Matthew about prayer. In verses 9–13, Matthew quotes Jesus telling us how we should pray by teaching us what has become commonly known as the Lord's Prayer.

> And when you pray, do not be like the hypocrites,
> for they love to pray standing in the synagogues

and on the street corners to be seen by others. Truly I tell you, they have received their reward in full. But when you pray, go into your room, close the door and pray to your Father, who is unseen. Then your Father, who sees what is done in secret, will reward you. And when you pray, do not keep on babbling like pagans, for they think they will be heard because of their many words. Do not be like them, for your Father knows what you need before you ask him.

Now the Lord's Prayer beginning in verse 9.

This, then, is how you should pray:

Our Father in heaven, hallowed be your name, your kingdom come, your will be done, on earth as it is in heaven. Give us today our daily bread. And forgive us our debts as we also have forgiven our debtors. And lead us not into temptation but deliver us from the evil one.

For if you forgive other people when they sin against you, your heavenly Father will also forgive you. But if you do not forgive others their sins, your Father will not forgive your sins. (Matthew 5:5–15)

I would like to add here that you might notice the Lord's Prayer that Jesus taught us ends with "But deliver us from the evil one." The modern version of this prayer also adds to the original prayer, "For thine is the kingdom and the power and the glory forever and ever. Amen."

About fasting:

When you fast, do not look somber as the hyp-ocrites do, for they disfigure their faces to show others they are fasting. Truly I tell you, they have received their reward in full. But when you fast, put oil on your head and wash your face, so that it will not be obvious to others that you are fasting, but only to your Father, who is unseen; and your Father, who sees what is done in secret, will reward you. (Matthew 5:16–18)

About treasures:

Do not store up your selves treasures on earth, where moths and vermin destroy, and where thieves break in and steal. But store up for yourselves treasures in heaven, where moths and vermin do not destroy, and where thieves do not break in and steal. For where your treasure is, there your heart will be also.

The eye is the lamp of the body. If your eyes are healthy your whole body will be full of light. But if your eyes are unhealthy, your whole body will be full of darkness. If then the light within you is darkness, how great is that darkness!

No one can serve two masters. Either you will hate the one and love the other, or you will be devoted to the one and despise the other. You cannot serve both God and money. (Matthew 6:19–24)

In the Bible, Jesus's lesson about treasures is combined with the eyes being the lamp of the body. This is very confusing to new Christians. My personal opinion is that these are two separate lessons.

About the eyes being the lamp of the body:

The eye is the lamp of the body. If your eyes are healthy, your whole body will be full of light. But if your eyes are unhealthy, your whole body will be full of darkness. If then the light within you is darkness, how great is that darkness!

About serving two masters, God or money:

No one can serve two masters. Either you will hate the one and love the other, or you will be devoted to the one and despise the other. You cannot serve both God and money.

This second lesson is easier to understand. You should not love money. If you take in money and not tithe or help the needy but keep most of your income to yourself, you are being selfish. It is really not your money after all. All things on this earth belong to God. Even the Cherokee culture believes that the wife owns the home, but nobody can own the land. For the Creator created the land, and therefore, it belongs to him and him alone. When you came into the world, you came in naked and without anything. When you leave this world, you will leave in exactly the same way. Therefore, do not treat your income as something belonging to you as though you can take it with you when you pass away.

Many denominations teach that it is a sin to be rich. They quote what Jesus told the rich man, "It is easier for a camel to pass through the eye of a needle than for a rich man to enter into heaven." He also states, "If you want to enter heaven, sell all your belongings and follow me."

At this, the rich man left. He was not willing to follow Jesus if that meant he had to give up all his money.

What most denominations teach is that Jesus is saying if you love your money so much that you are not willing to give it up to follow him, then you are guilty of serving your money as your god and not the heavenly Father.

About worry, I will not quote the entire lesson but give you the most important issues to store in your memory. You are not to worry about what to wear or what to eat. Here is what Jesus says concerning worry about what you will eat or drink and also about what you will wear.

> Look at the birds of the air; they do not sow or reap or store away in barns, and yet your heavenly Father feeds them. Are you not much more valuable than they? Can any one of you by worrying add a single hour to your life?
>
> So do not worry, saying, "What shall we eat?" Or "What shall we drink?" or "what shall we wear?" For the pagans run after all these things, and your heavenly Father knows that you need them. But seek first his kingdom and his righteousness, and all these things will be given to you as well. Therefore do not worry about tomorrow, for tomorrow will worry about itself. Each day has enough trouble of its own. (Matthew 6:25–27, 31–34)

About judging others, I now summarize rather than quote Jesus in its entirety: We shall not judge others, for it is only our heavenly Father who has the right to judge. However, when we see a brother or sister doing something they should not do, we can bring it to their attention but not in a judging way. Rather, we should do so in a loving way, for Jesus commanded us to "love each other."

About being proud, here are several lessons concerning being proud.

> Do not be proud, but be willing to associate with people of low position. Do not be conceited. (Romans 12:16)

First Corinthians 13:4 combines both the rule of not being proud along with what love is: "Love is patient, love is kind. It does not envy, it does not boast, it is not proud. It does not dishonor others, it is not self-seeking, it is not easily angered, it keeps no record of wrongs. Love does not delight in evil but rejoices with the truth. It always protects, always trusts, always hopes, always perseveres."

> People will be lovers of themselves, lovers of money boastful, proud, abusive, disobedient to their parents, ungrateful, unholy, without love, unforgiving, slanderous, without self-control, brutal, not lovers of the good, treacherous, rash, conceited, lovers of pleasure rather than lovers of God—having a form of godliness but denying its power. Have nothing to do with such people. (2 Timothy 3:2–5)

> God opposes the proud but shows favor to the humble. (James 4:6)

> In the same way, you who are younger, submit yourselves to your elders. All of you, clothe yourselves with humility toward one another, because, "God opposes the proud but shows favor to the humble. (1 Peter 5:5)

There is one very important lesson which is being played out in our current times. It is about Israel and the Jewish people. Remember what God promised Abram before he renamed him Abraham. God is quoted speaking to Abram in Genesis 12: "I will make you into a great nation, and I will bless you; I will make your name great, and you will be a blessing. I will bless those who bless you, and whoever curses you I will curse; and all peoples on earth will be blessed through you."

The lessons which come directly from the Holy Bible are those which we, who are the children of light, must try our best to be mindful.

There is one thing above all that must be kept in mind. We are to live each day with God in our minds and in both our thoughts and our actions. To do this takes time. It will not all fall into place in one instant. However, I have some suggestions. I will take all the lessons intended for all children of light and shorten them down to as few words as possible. By reading these words, you can keep as much of these lessons in our heads at all times. The book of Proverbs in the Old Testament gives one very important lesson which is written by Solomon under the inspiration of God. We must seek wisdom. Then we must keep wisdom in our hearts because God looks into the hearts of both the righteous and the unrighteous looking to see if wisdom is there. With wisdom comes knowledge.

Remember also what comes out of our mouth comes from the heart. If hatefulness comes out of our mouth, then that is what is in our heart. If evil comes out of our mouth, then evil is what in in our heart.

About turning away from God and risk of losing one's salvation:

If you are guilty of turning to the world where things of the flesh are things that replace God in your hearts, you must suffer God's wrath. This is probably one of the most important lessons children of light must keep in their hearts and not be tempted to let go or turn away from these lessons.

We must strive to be more like Jesus. One common phrase used to accomplish this is to ask ourselves, "What would Jesus do?" If we keep God in our thoughts throughout every day and try to do exactly what Jesus would do, we are in a kind of spiritual state and in constant communication with the Holy Trinity: God the Father, God the Son, and God the Holy Spirit.

Here now are those key words to keep in our minds at all times:

Blessed are the poor in spirit, those who morn, the meek, those who hunger and thirst for righteousness, those who are merciful, those who are pure in heart, the peacemakers, those persecuted because of righteousness.

You are the light of the world. Shine your light so others can see the ways of the Lord.

Never call someone empty-headed or a fool.

Obey the Ten Commandments (short version):

1. You shall have no other gods before me.
2. You shall not make an image in the form of anything in heaven or on earth.

3. You shall not misuse the name of the Lord your God.
4. Remember the Sabbath day and keep it holy.
5. Honor your father and your mother.
6. You shall not murder.
7. You shall not commit adultery.
8. You shall not steal.
9. You shall not give false testimony against your neighbor.
10. You shall not covet your neighbor's house, wife, servants, ox, donkey, or anything that belongs to your neighbor.

Divorce only for reasons of sexual immorality or hardened heart and unwilling to change.

About taking oaths (this one is dependent on your denomination):

God intended marriage between male and female in order to be as one flesh and populate the world.

Do not live in sin with sex outside of marriage. Do not experiment as a couple to see if you should then get married.

Give to the needy in secret.

Pray in secret—unless in worship when two or more are gathered in the Lord's name.

Fast in secret.

God knows your needs. Do not worry about your needs. God will provide.

Memorize the Lord's Prayer, which Jesus taught us.

Treasures should be about those in heaven. Do not store great wealth on earth.

The eyes are the lamp of the body. They tell the health of the body.

Serve God as your master, not money. One cannot serve two masters.

Do not judge others. Only God has the right to judge.

Do not be proud and boast about yourself.

Seek wisdom, and keep it in your heart so God will see that you have wisdom (Proverbs).

What comes out of your mouth is what is in your heart. If evil or hatred comes out of your mouth, then that is what is in your heart.

Jesus's final command is to simply "love each other."

Keep God and Jesus in your mind all through the day, and do not turn away from them for the pleasures of the flesh and the dark world which is the world ruled by Satan.

I sincerely hope that this shortened list of twenty-two things is helpful to new Christians upon being born again and becoming one of God's children—children of light. Those who have been one of the children of light for some time can use these twenty-two items as a reminder of what is expected of you. Go over them daily or several times a week. There is one thing that all Christians are supposed to do: read/study the Bible at least fifteen minutes a day. If you have a family, it is good for all members to attend a Bible reading or Bible study session each day.

If you wish to remain one of those known as the children of light, you must turn away from the dark, and do not turn away from God. You must keep God as number one in your hearts. You must glorify God. "If you glorify the things of the world you will de-glorify God and God will not keep you and you will die." You must live in the Spirit and stay full of God. God must be on your mind every hour of every day. Do not let the other things in daily life cause you to stumble and put God out of your hearts. If you allow yourself to stray away from keeping God as number one in your heart, you must suffer the wrath of God. I do not wish to cause you pain. There is a solution if you are guilty of straying away from God. As Jesus said, "Leave your sinful ways," and then repent with true sincerity, and ask for God to allow you back in his grace. God will take you back. But as long as you continue to enjoy the things of the flesh and harden your hearts to God, you will not see the kingdom of God. Keep the things written above about losing one's salvation.

I have one final suggestion. The Christian Broadcasting Network (CBN) offers a series of lessons for children. It is called the *Superbook*. It is good for children to learn many of these lessons at an early age. They will then retain that knowledge so that obeying the lessons of God and his only Son, Jesus, is much easier.

Those families that attend church together, pray together, and read the Bible together not only tend to stay together; but they are a shining beacon of light for all the world to see. Yes, those who live in the dark world will hate you. But is it not better to have the evil ones hate you rather than have God displeased with you? For those of the dark world also hate Jesus and God. They will not ever see the kingdom of God according to the scriptures of the Holy Bible.

CHAPTER 9

Who Are to Become Prophets?

God has been teaching me and guiding me all of my life to become what he wants of me. He has a plan for each individual. His first words to me via a telepathic message were that I am to *"enlighten others in an entertaining way."* God gave me musical talent way back when I was a child. I became an accomplished musician and then a singer/songwriter/musician. God used that gift to have me write songs for him which were produced onto CDs which I give away for free. The songs of the first CD were given to me in the middle of the night in the form of a new melody which God replayed over and over in my head. Then he would have me go to my music room and write down some form of music notation so as to not forget the melody the next morning. Following that, God would direct me to a scripture which would be used as the topic for the song's lyrics.

Part of my teaching was to attend various churches of different denominations so I could compare their similarities and their differences. I mentioned earlier that God also had me join, along with my wife, a nondenominational church. I discovered that these churches are more like the early churches which were started just after Jesus returned to be with his Father in heaven. There was no governing body that dictated what their preachers should and should not preach. Nondenominational preachers are to simply preach from the Bible. As much as humanly possible, they are to back up anything they preach by quoting the scriptures from which they derived their sermon or talk, or even a book like this one.

My work in writing all my books required much research time in the Bible to be sure I did not add nor subtract anything from the scriptures. The same goes for the writing of sermons. Like the books, these sermons were also God inspired. My first seven sermons were written in just a few days in preparation for my first preaching assignment as an ordained independent minister, more commonly called a nondenominational preacher.

Our heavenly Father now has me writing books for him which is also a form of entertainment. He also has changed my hobby of painting landscapes into painting landscapes that are based on scriptures. The scriptures are to be quoted and appear somewhere in the paintings. I do work on this assignment while my books are in the hands of my publisher.

At the same time I was working on writing the books and painting scripture-based landscapes, God wanted me to return to my music. This time I was to complete some Christian songs I had begun writing years ago but never finished. He also wanted me to use what I learned as a pastor and the research required in the writing of sermons to come up with the scriptures to use as the lyrics for additional songs and publish a second CD.

Now that you know the background, it is time to move on to the next step in my assignments. Without me realizing it, God has chosen me to be a prophet. I am not the only one. God is producing many new prophets because there is a reason for him wanting to get his words out to the people more than he has in the past. Therefore, I am not one of few but one of many.

God knows which of his human creations will ultimately be given the assignment to be a prophet. Yes, when I looked back at my writing of God's books, I realized I was passing onto God's children those things he wishes them to know. They may or may not include things that will happen in the future. However, they are all things God wants to have passed down to those he considers his. I also believe he wants those who live in the dark to possibly listen and learn what God expects of them as well. Remember, God loves all of those he created—both the righteous and the unrighteous. He knows what is in the hearts of both the righteous and the unrighteous.

The prophets in the Old Testament passed on the people what God wanted them to know. They did this in either of two ways. They would stand in the streets and tell those around what God wants them to know. He also had them put his words into writing which ultimately became books of the Old Testament. Now God instructed me to put his messages to the people in words in the books he has me writing. Therefore, according to God, I am a prophet. I called my publisher to find out if other authors found themselves in the same situation. I was told that some authors actually put the title of prophet in front of their name on their books instead of simply *Pastor*. This is how I know that God now has many prophets and is trying to get his word out via these many new prophets.

Therefore, there are probably going to be more prophets working at the same time more than ever before. God is now pouring out his Spirit upon the earth like never before, and this pouring out of his Spirit includes the writings of his prophets.

CHAPTER 10

Where Do We Go from Here?

Using what God has been telling me about our current culture and learning all the events happening in the world, I truly believe we are in the end days. Soon the world will come to an end as we know it. I can also observe Satan pouring out demonic spirits onto the people of the world especially the righteous to try to get all who will listen to his teaching to come to him. He loves for humans to worship him. He does not love the humans that worship him, though. In fact, he does not love anything God, our Father in heaven, created.

There is one exception. God created Lucifer or Satan, and he loves himself. Jesus said he is the father of all lies. Here is the scripture to back up that statement.

> If God were your Father, you would love me, for I have come here from God. I have not come on my own; God sent me. Why is my language not clear to you? Because you are not able to hear what I say. You belong to your father, the devil, and you want to carry out your father's desires. He was a murderer from the beginning, not holding to the truth, for there is no truth in him. When he lies, he speaks his native language, for he is a liar and the father of lies. (John 8:43–44)

Satan uses lies to get people to turn away from God. He especially takes great pleasure in trying to win over those who are born-again Christians. These are among God's favorite children, and Satan wants to hurt God where it hurts the most—convincing God's children of light to come to him.

To battle this onslaught from Satan, God is also pouring out his Spirit upon the earth even as I write his books for him. He is teaching more of his children to become disciples and also prophets. In this the way, they can be used to combat Satan's trickery. There are many who will listen. I believe that it is God's pouring out of his Spirit that has caused the people of Iran to recently becoming Christians by the tens of thousands. There are other countries whereby American and Israeli Christians are converting people to Christianity.

The Christian Broadcasting Network, CBN, is drilling wells so that thousands of children are no longer dying each day from drinking polluted water. They are helping the poor people of villages around the world to be more self-sufficient. They set them up in business for themselves so they can earn a living and are now able to support their families. Because of this activity, they are winning many over to become Christians. If being a Christian means doing all the great things that CBN and other organizations do, then they want to be a part of it.

I do believe that God is teaching me that soon there will be a definite split between those who are with God and those who are with Satan. We will soon see the future which was foretold by Jesus to John in spirit in the book of Revelation. The word *revelation* means the act of revealing something. In this case, since neither Jesus nor his Father can lie that reveling is the truth. Jesus said this in the book of John.

"Jesus answered, 'I am the way and the truth and the life. No one comes to the Father except through me. If you really know me, you will know my Father as well. From now on you know him and have seen him'" (John 14:6–7).

God wants as many of his creation to come to him—whether they live in the light and are born-again Christians or they now live in the dark but are willing to listen to the teachings of the preachers, disciples, and prophets and turn away from the dark and try to find out what pleases the Lord. They want to become Christians. As I just explained earlier God is pouring out his Spirit and wants to win over as many of his creation to be with him in heaven. Yet like Jesus told the disciples when they encountered those who would not listen to their teachings, they should shake off the dust from their sandals and move on. We cannot save everyone even though that is exactly what we hope to do. We certainly do not want our culture to be part of that which is turning toward the dark world of Satan.

Many who now live in the dark world headed by Satan are becoming Christians by their own free will. You see, God has a rule that he does not mess with our free will which he gave to the humans he created. Instead he relies on the works of his preachers, disciples, and prophets to accomplish this swaying of their free will to want to be with God rather than with Satan.

Unfortunately, there are those in the dark world who fell very hard for Satan's trickery. They were once born again children of light but decided by their own free will to turn away from God. In a sermon by Dr. Charles Stanley, he stated that Satan loves to dwell on a person's desires and convinces them to go ahead with those desires even if they are considered sins.

As I explained in an earlier chapter, those who were once born-again Christians who committed such sins such as murder, theft, sexual immorality, and such caused God to turn them over to their lust and exit their bodies. Think about what I just wrote. If they were once born again and then God, because of their horrible sinfulness, turns them over to their lusts, then they are lost children. To me, that means he is done with them unless they repent and ask for forgiveness. But for now, they are turned over to Satan and will be under the control and influence of Satan and his demons. In fact, as I quoted earlier, the book of Romans explains about God accepting the lost souls back into his good graces if they repent and stop committing those horrible sins.

If they fail to repent, their bodies are no longer God's temple, and God no longer is in those people. Satan instantly moves in to fill that void. The sinners then under Satan's influence rationalize by making statements that are contrary to scripture. They decide what scriptures they are willing to agree with and those they feel are false. God does not lie, so every word in the Bible is God inspired regardless of who the author is. The Bible is the truth and must be taken seriously. There should be no deciding as to which passages are to be believed and which ones not.

Because God cannot lie, he would not tell the person to go ahead and commit sins. He would not tell them that what they are doing is acceptable according to our current culture and that anyone who disagrees with what they are doing has the problems and not the person committing the sin. Only Satan would say such statements.

If God has turned them over to their lusts, then he has turned them over to the teachings of Satan, and God will step aside until such time as they repent for their sins and ask God for forgiveness and, most importantly, discontinue committing those sins.

As a nondenominational pastor, disciple, and prophet, I want to assure you that I do my best to never add nor subtract anything quoted in the Bible. However, along with preaching from the Bible, I listen closely for input from God. When I write these books, I am in constant two-way spiritual communication with our Father in heaven. You can choose not to believe me, but in trying to be more like Jesus and God, I do not lie. If I say something that later turns out to be untrue, I will talk to those with whom I said those things and explain that when I said them I believed them with all my heart to be the truth. I apologize and ask them to forgive me for my mistake. I then tell them the truth of which I was not previously aware.

These scriptures tell us that he is turning those who commit sexual immorality over to their lust and that they will have no inheritance in the kingdom of Christ and of God. If the kingdom of Christ and God means heaven, then they will not be allowed in heaven. If they are not allowed to be in heaven, then they must be with Satan. If they ask to be forgiven and leave their sinful ways, God will welcome them back as one of his own once again.

I now quote from Revelation 21:7–8, "Those who are victorious will inherit all this, and I will be their God and they will be my children. But the cowardly, the unbelieving, the vile, the murderers the sexually immoral, those who practice magic arts, the idolaters and all liars—they will be consigned to the fiery lake of burning sulfur. This is the second death."

That statement in the book of Revelation makes it clear that they will be going into the lake of burning sulfur. That means hell along with Satan. They followed Satan's guidance and listened to his lies and fell for his lies. Everyone must be aware of how to best battle the influence of Satan and his demons. The best way to do this is to not only read the Bible regularly but believe every word for every word was inspired by God. To not believe what God inspired to be written, then they are calling God a liar. That, my dear friends, is not the righteous way to live. To have one's desired pleasures that are considered serious sins by God and his Son for the short time they are on this earth is nothing compared to what they will suffer for eternity. That is not a good trade. Anyone with common sense should learn this lesson from the Bible and do their best to be more like Jesus. Jesus would never do the things that are mentioned in the scriptures quoted above.

It is written that Satan and his demons hate God and all he created. This especially includes humans, for Satan knows each human; he studies each of us in order to know our weaknesses and our desires. He then uses that knowledge to attack us at our weakest points.

There is more to be quoted from Revelation. That book is extremely important because it reveals much more than what is written in the preceding books of the Bible. There are more very important lessons for all of us to read and know.

> Yet, I hold this against you: You have forsaken the love you had at first. Consider how far you have fallen! Repent and do the things you did at first. If you do not repent, I will come to you and remove your lampstand from its place. (Revelation 2:4–5)

> Nevertheless, I have a few things against you: There are some among you who hold to the

teaching of Balaam. Who taught Balak to entice
the Israelites to sin so that they ate food sacrificed to idols and committed sexual immorality.
Likewise, you also have those who hold to the
teachings of the Nicolaitans. Repent therefore.
(Revelation 2:14–16)

I now offer additional evidence concerning those who live by
the flesh and partake in sexual immorality.

Here are my final words on the subject of sexual immorality.
The two words "sexual immorality" or sexually immoral" are listed in
the Holy Bible forty-three times. It is often mentioned in the same
verse as adulterers, murders, the practice of evil arts, and many more
unclean acts that will cause the guilty party to either not be allowed
in heaven or have turned away from God. God is in charge. God is
the head of his kingdom. He has a perfect right to say who he will
allow in his kingdom and who will not be allowed.

The preachers, pastors, ministers, reverends, or such other people who are often referred to as men of God cannot, in my understanding of the Bible, be a one of God's teachers. If they have committed such a great sin as to no longer be in God and God will
no longer be in them, then how can they be among those who are
permitted to enter the kingdom of God when they leave this earth?

Remember, God never turns away from those who are his children, the children of light, because they live in the light. If a child
of God chooses, by their own free will, to turn away from God and
prefer to live in the dark world which is headed by Satan and his
demonic beings, then they, the children who *lived* in the light, are
now *part of and live in the dark world with the evildoers.*

Yet they are not lost completely if they take it upon themselves
to be back in God's good graces. They can be with God once more.
They can confess their sins of the dark world and ask for God's forgiveness one more time. We all know that as being called *repent.* God
loves them, but they have shown that they no longer love God. God
will accept them back if they truly want to come back to God with all
their hearts, all their souls, and all their minds. That means, though,

that they must give up their evil lifestyle and go back to acting like children of light once more.

So that you don't think I am making all this up, I now list the most important entries which put sexual immorality in with the other major sins and what God has to say about them.

First Corinthians 5:9 through 6:9 contain such entries as,

> I wrote to you in my letter not to associate with sexually immoral people—not at all meaning the people of this world who are immoral, or the greedy and swindlers, or idolaters. In that case you would have to leave this world. But now I am writing to you that you must not associate with anyone who claims to be a brother or sister but is sexually immoral or greedy, and idolater or slanderer, a drunkard or swindler. Do not even eat with such people.
>
> What business is it of mine to judge those outside the church? Are you not to judge those inside? God will judge those outside. "Expel the wicked person from among you."

Then in verse 6:9, Paul writes, "Or do you not know that wrongdoers will not inherit the kingdom of God? Do not be deceived: Neither the sexually immoral nor idolaters nor adulterers nor men who have sex with men nor thieves nor the greedy nor drunkards nor slanderers nor swindlers will inherit the kingdom of God."

I would like to mention now that Paul continues with a complete lesson on sexual immorality beginning with 6:12–20, which concludes chapter 6. In order to keep this chapter short, I will now suggest that you read those verses just mentioned in 1 Corinthians 6.

Ephesians 5:3 states, "But among you there must not be even a hint of sexual immorality, or of any kind of impurity, or of greed because these are improper for God's holy people."

In Ephesians 5:5, it is written, "For of this you can be sure; No immoral, impure or greedy person—such a person is an idolater—has any inheritance in the kingdom of Christ and of God."

In 1 Timothy 1:9, it is written, "We also know that the law is made not for the righteous but the for the lawbreakers and rebels, the ungodly and sinful, the unholy and irreligious, for those who kill their fathers or mothers, for murderers, for the sexually immoral, for those practicing homosexuality, for slave traders and liars and perjurers—and for whatever else is contrary to the sound doctrine that conforms to the gospel concerning the glory of the blessed God, which he entrusted to me."

Hebrews 12:16 says, "See that no one is sexually immoral, or is godless like Esau, who from a single meal sold his inheritance rights as the oldest son."

And in Hebrews 13:4, it says, "Marriage should be honored by all, and the marriage bed kept pure, for God will judge the adulterer and all the sexually immoral."

Revelation 21:7–8 says, "Those who are victorious will inherit all this, and I will be their God and they will be my children. But the cowardly, the unbelieving, the vile, the murderers, the sexually immoral, those who practice magic arts, the idolaters and all liars— they will be consigned to the fiery lake of burning sulfur. This is the second death"

In Revelation 22:14–15, Jesus himself also states, "Blessed are those who wash their robes, that they may have the right to the tree of life and may go through the gates into the city. Outside are the dogs, those who practice magic arts, the sexually immoral, the murderers, the idolaters and everyone who loves and practices falsehood."

Even in the Old Testament, we find in Numbers 25:1 this statement: "While Israel was staying in Shittim, the men began to indulge in sexual immorality with Moabite women who invited them to the sacrifices to their gods. The people ate the sacrificial meal and bowed down before these gods. So, Israel yoked themselves to the Baal of Peor. And the Lord's anger burned against them."

In Matthew 5:32, Jesus said this: "But I tell you that anyone who divorces his wife except for sexual immorality, makes her the victim of adultery, and anyone who marries a divorced woman commits adultery."

In Matthew 15:19, Jesus also says, "For out of the heart comes evil thoughts—murder, adultery, sexual immorality, theft, false testimony, slander. These are what defile a person; but eating with unwashed hands does not defile them."

In Matthew 19:9, Jesus says, "I tell you that anyone who divorces his wife except for sexual immorality, and marries another woman commits adultery."

In Mark 7:21–23, Jesus is once more speaking: "For it is from within, out of a person's heart, that evil thoughts come—sexual immorality, theft, murder, adultery, greed, malice, deceit, lewdness, envy, slander, arrogance and folly. All these evils come from inside and defile a person."

I would like to remind you that in the book of Acts the Holy Spirit, one-third of the Holy Trinity descended upon the disciples and gave them the same powers that Jesus had while he was among us on earth. Therefore, anything that is written in the letters to Churches and other audiences hold the same truth and power as if Jesus said them. We are told by the evildoers that since Jesus did not specifically say they should not commit homosexuality that it is okay to do so. However, as you just read in some of the above scriptures, it was Jesus himself who said the same things about sexual immorality.

Therefore, in Acts 15:19–21, we read, "It is my judgment, therefore, that we should not make it difficult for the Gentiles who are turning to God. Instead we should write to them, telling them to abstain from food polluted by idols, from sexual immorality, from the eating of strangled animals and from blood. For the law of Moses has been preached in every city from the earliest times and is read in the synagogues on every Sabbath."

In Acts 15:29, we read, "You are to abstain from food sacrificed to idols, from blood, from the meat of strangled animals and from sexual immorality. You will do well to avoid these things."

Finally, in Acts 21:25, we read, "As for the Gentile believers, we have written to them our decision that they should abstain from food sacrificed to idols, from blood, from the meat of strangled animals and from sexual immorality."

I do realize that in the book of Acts, there are things that are repetitious, but if that be the case, then it must be because it is of the utmost importance and we should be aware that it is of the utmost importance.

In Romans, there is only one mention of sexual immorality. Romans 13:13–14 says, "Let us behave decently, as in the daytime, not in carousing and drunkenness, not in sexual immorality and debauchery, not in dissension and jealousy. Rather clothe yourselves with the Lord Jesus Christ, and do not think about how to gratify the desires of the flesh."

That is an extremely powerful scripture!

In 1 Corinthians 5:1, Paul writes, "It is actually reported that there is sexual immorality among you, and of a kind that even pagans do not tolerate: A man is sleeping with his father's wife."

First Corinthians 6:13 says, "You say, 'Food for the stomach and the stomach for food, and God will destroy them both.' The body, however, is not meant for sexual immorality but for the Lord, and the Lord for the body."

First Corinthians 6:18–19 says, "Flee from sexual immorality. All other sins a person commits are outside the body, but whoever sins sexually, sins against their own body. Do you not know that your bodies are temples of the Holy Spirit, who is in you, whom you have received from God? You are not your own; you were bought at a price. Therefore, honor God with your bodies."

First Corinthians 7:2 says, "But since sexual immorality is occurring, each man should have sexual relations with his own wife, and each woman with her own husband."

First Corinthians 10:8–9 says, "We should not commit sexual immorality, as some of them did—and in one day twenty-three thousand of them died. We should not test Christ, as some of them did—and were killed by snakes."

Galatians 5:19 says, "The acts of the flesh are obvious; sexual immorality, impurity and debauchery; idolatry and witchcraft; hatred discord, jealousy, fits of rage, selfish ambition, dissensions, factions and envy; drunkenness, orgies, and the like. I warn you, as I did before, that those who live like this will not inherit the kingdom of God."

Colossians 3:5–10 says, "Put to death, therefore whatever belongs to your earthly nature; sexual immorality, impurity, lust, evil desires and greed, which is idolatry. Because of these, the wrath of God is coming. You used to walk in these ways, in the life you once lived. But now you must also rid yourselves of all such things as filthy language from your lips. Do not lie to each other, since you have taken off your old self with its practices and have put on the new self, which is being renewed in knowledge in the image of its Creator."

First Thessalonians 4:3–6 says, "It is God's will that you should be sanctified; that you should avoid sexual immorality; that each of you should learn to control your own body in a way that is holy and honorable, not in passionate lust like the pagans, who do not know God; and that in this matter no one should wrong or take advantage of a brother or sister."

Jude 4 says, "For certain individuals whose condemnation was written about long ago have secretly slipped in among you. They are ungodly people, who pervert the grace of our God into a license for immorality and deny Jesus Christ our only Sovereign and Lord."

Jude 7 says, "In a similar way, Sodom and Gomorrah and the surrounding towns gave themselves up to sexual immorality and per-version. They serve as an example of those who suffer the punishment of eternal fire."

You cannot get any plainer that that! It states in simple to understand language that those who insist on continuing their ways of sexual immorality risk suffering the same ending as those who committed sexual immorality in Sodom and Gomorrah and their surrounding towns. God destroyed them.

In Revelation, there are four different references to sexual immorality. Three of them are in chapter 2 and one in chapter 9.

In Revelation 2:14–21, Jesus is speaking to John, whom he brought up into heaven via Spirit,

> Nevertheless, I have a few things against you: There are some among you who hold to the teaching of Balaam, who taught Balak to entice the Israelites to sin so that they ate food sacrificed to

idols and committed sexual immorality. Likewise, you also have those who hold to the teaching of the Nicolaitans. Repent therefore! Otherwise, I will soon come to you and will fight against them with the sword of my mouth. Whoever has ears, let them hear what the Spirit says to the churches. To the one who is victorious, I will give some of the hidden manna. I will also give that person a white stone with a new name written on it, known only to the one who receives it.

To the angel of the church of Thyatira write:

These are the words of the Son of God, whose eyes are like blazing fire and whose feet are like burnished bronze. I know your deeds, your love and faith, your service and perseverance, and that you are now doing more than you did at first. Nevertheless, I have this against you: You tolerate that woman Jezebel, who calls herself a prophet. By her teaching she misleads my servants into sexual immorality and the eating of food sacrificed to idols. I have given her time to repent of her immorality, but she is unwilling.

Revelation 9:21 says, "Nor did they repent of their murders, their magic arts, their sexual immorality or their thefts."

I would now like to introduce my readers to a very important passage in the Bible that does not use the term "sexual immorality" but deals with the subject matter very boldly. In the book of Romans, Paul wrote to the Church in Rome under the heading "God's Wrath against Sinful Humanity."

Paul writes these words in Romans 1:26–32,

Because of this, God gave them over to shameful lusts. Even their women exchanged natural sexual relations for unnatural ones. In the same way the men also abandoned natural relations with women and were inflamed with lust for one another. Men committed shameful acts with other men, and received in themselves the due penalty for their error.

Furthermore, just as they did not think it worthwhile to retain the knowledge of God, so God gave them over to a depraved mind, so that they do what ought not to be done. They have become filled with every kind of wickedness, evil, greed and depravity. They are full of envy, murder, strife, deceit and malice. They are gossips, slanderers, God-haters, insolent arrogant and boastful; they invent ways of doing evil; they disobey their parents; they have no understanding, no fidelity, no love, no mercy. Although they know Gods righteous decree that those who do such things deserve death, they not only continue to do these very things but also approve of those who practice them.

I think I have pointed out what the scriptures have to say about sexual immorality. Now you can compare what is quoted above with what is happening in our culture. Movies, television shows, product commercials, and even cartoons are openly displaying sexual immorality almost constantly. It is hard to find even one show or movie or commercial that does not join in with the evil culture into which we are beginning to evolve. That is a shame. How can we also pass laws that state we are not to discriminate against such evil. It was quoted from the scriptures above that we are to have nothing to do with such people, yet our culture and laws are demanding we not only accept them but to accept the evil acts that they commit.

This, my dear friends, is my final word on the subject. May God bless you, and may his inspired words in this book help to fight against the evil culture we are now becoming. Do not be fooled into thinking that this new way of thinking is the right way or is completely acceptable. As a nondenominational preacher, I do not believe in gay or lesbian pastors in our churches. I preach strictly from the Bible, and if you do not like my preaching, then you also do not like the teachings of the Bible. There is no question about it; you must obey God and his only Son, Christ Jesus. For your own sake, please do so. If you have strayed away the biblical quotations which are mentioned above, please remember that you do have one last chance. *You must repent.* God loves you and so do I. I pray for those who have not yet seen the light and have been fooled into thinking by false teachers that what they are doing is not against God. What they are doing is against God. For the Bible tells us so.

Because God loves you, he wants you to come back and welcome him once more into your body, his temple. He, Jesus, and the Holy Spirit will readily return if you repent and turn away from the dark world which is headed by Satan and his demonic beings—the fallen angles who left heaven with him.

> Therefore, there is now no condemnation for those who are in Christ Jesus, because through Christ Jesus the law of the Spirit who gives life has set you free from the law of sin and death. For what the law was powerless to do because it was weakened by the flesh. God did by sending his own Son in the likeness of sinful flesh to be a sin offering. And so, he condemned sin in the flesh, in order that the righteous requirement of the law might be fully met in us who do not live according to the flesh but according to the Spirit.
>
> Those who live according to the flesh have their minds set on what the flesh desires; but those who live in accordance with the Spirit have their minds set on what the Spirit desires. The mind governed by the flesh is death, but the mind governed by the Spirit is life and peace. The mind governed by the flesh is hostile to God; it

does not submit to God's law nor can it do so.
Those who are in the realm of the flesh cannot
please God. (Romans 8:1–8)

Upon trying to minister to those who live by the flesh and commit the sin of sexual immorality which God despises, I discovered that what is written in Romans 8 is very true. Those who insist in living in the flesh seem to rationalize that what they are doing is acceptable and in no way against God. I believe that they are listening to either Satan or his demonic spirits who tell them that what they are doing is not against God and that those who want nothing to do with them because of their actions have the problem and not themselves.

There are preachers, disciples, and prophets who try to tell them they are headed down the wrong path and they no longer enjoy God's presence. But Satan, who loves to pretend to be God, has stepped in and occupied that space that God used to call his temple. He tells the person that what they are doing is perfectly okay. They should continue doing what they are doing because they will be forgiven of their sins as God promised. Another lie from the father of lies.

To make matters even worse, if that is possible, there are preachers who are guilty of sexual immorality. They, like their other human counterparts, have turned away from God and practice sexual immorality as though it is the right thing to do even though scripture tells us that God detests murder, theft, and sexual immorality and all the other serious sins mentioned in the scriptures quoted earlier. Children in the churches are being molested by preachers of all denominations. This is not new. It has been going on for a very long time. That means to me that the end days began a long time ago. Or at least Satan has been pouring out his evil spirits onto unsuspecting Christians, including the members of the clergy.

Where we go from here is up to each individual. If we are to be a nation blessed by God, then we need to not only acknowledge God but learn from his inspired words. If we fail to do this and our culture turns away from God in favor of evilness, then we risk not being blessed by God any longer. The next chapter will tell us more details about what will happen if we do not succeed in changing the direction of our current culture. It is now turning away from God, and that is a very dangerous thing to be doing. Please use whatever power you have to battle Satan. As it states in Ephesians, "Put on your full armor of God."

Let there be light, and may that light shine on what is the truth.

CHAPTER 11

What Happens if We Do Not Succeed?

Let me begin by informing you that when I completed chapter 10, I thought that was the end of this book. Then I was awakened by our Father in heaven with a vision. This is only the third vision from God that I have experienced. The vision just before this one is when I found out from God that I was now one of many prophets God will work through to inform the people of those things that are about to happen. Like the prophets in the Old Testament, I, too, am receiving messages from God that he wants to be written so that everyone will have a chance to know what God wants and what he wants us to do, what he wants us to become, and what he wants in order for our country to continue to be blessed by him.

The vision was one of my computer screens. It was as though I had just turned on my computer, and it went straight to the word-processing software, and on the blank page, it said, "What Happens if We Do Not Succeed?" I put on my robe and received a message from God about the first thing that will happen if we fail to keep this country one that is based on righteousness, the truth, and all that is good under God's guidance. He said that he will no longer bless this nation if our culture continues down its current path. I thought that even though God has been telling me I am one of many new prophets, I have yet to receive a telepathic message from him telling me something about the future. That suddenly changed upon receiving this latest vision. This chapter will include any and all things God tells me about what will happen if we do not succeed in blocking Satan's trickery to destroy our families, communities, churches, and governments at all levels.

Before continuing, I need to include several new messages from God concerning this subject. On the morning of September 16, 2019, Monday, I received a very strong feeling from God that I needed to listen to an interview in progress on CBN. It was the author of the new book *The Oracle*. It is a book that reveals prophecy from four thousand years ago about the country of Israel. In this book, it's said that it was prophesized that on December 6, 2017 a *trumpet* will sound, and the world would recognize Israel because one by one those who were persecuted elsewhere will come and worship the Lord on the holy mountain in Jerusalem. Notice that it was on that exact day that President Trump (as in trumpet) declared that the main embassy of the United States will no longer be in Tel Aviv. It is to be moved to Jerusalem, which is the biblical capital of Israel. It would be a specific day when calculated in Hebrew this date is exactly the date in which President Trump announced that the United States embassy would be moved from Tel Aviv to Jerusalem. The author being interviewed did not say which prophet foretold of this event, but as I searched, I found this prophecy as told in Isaiah 27:12–13: "In that day the LORD will thresh from the flowing Euphrates to the Wadi of Egypt, and you, Israel, will be gathered up one by one. And in that day a great trumpet will sound. Those who were perishing in Assyria and those who were exiled in Egypt will come and worship the LORD on the holy mountain in Jerusalem."

The author of this book also tells of the prophecy that the world, meaning the dark world of Satan in which we are not to love, will return to the way it was, as in paganism. Just as God inspired me to write about this very subject in his book you are now reading, he wanted me to include these two paragraphs so that if you want to know the truth it would be wise to purchase a copy of the book *The Oracle* just in case you have not done so yet. Now back to what was originally written before this latest message from God was received.

Those countries that burn churches and Bibles certainly cannot be blessed by God. It is obvious to many that those countries whose policies oppose the Ten Commandments, the teachings of Jesus, and the teachings of the apostles who were given the same powers as Jesus, as told in the book of Acts, are under the control of Satan. Why do you think that our leaders have consistently called those countries evil empires? The answer is simple. They practice evil which is what Satan does and teaches. God certainly is not evil, so it has to be the influence of the evil one, Satan. If we follow the path of those evil countries, we risk God no longer blessing our own country, the United States of America.

If we follow Satan's instructions on becoming a socialist nation that requires the government to be the god of the people, murder babies, or practice sexual immorality and all the other evil in the socialist agenda, we will not be blessed by God. I assure you that as a prophet, I have been told to express these things by God himself. God does not tolerate evilness at the level of individuals nor any government. Most who study the Bible know these things without having to be told by a prophet. Yet, even now, much of this is a common part of our current society's culture. Much of what I just mentioned is happening even now, and laws that favor these evil acts are being passed.

It must be stopped. If we are not able to stop this onslaught from Satan and his demonic army, we will be just like those other countries I just mentioned. God said, "Do not murder, steal, commit adultery, practice magic arts, or sexual immorality, among other evil acts." If our country opposes God, we will become like a third world country. Food will be scarce like it was under the Soviet Union. As many as seven families will be forced to share a small apartment like it was in the Soviet Union. If you attend a show by Yaakov Smirnov, you will know that all private companies will come under the ownership of the state. Companies owned by businesses based in foreign countries will be nationalized. *Nationalized* is the term used when the government of a country takes possession of all assets of a particular company. That company is considered nationalized.

That same thing will happen to all companies, foreign and domestic, that do business in the United States. The entire world will be in a state of chaos, and probably war will break out among many nations including our own. Those nations that still believe in obeying God will be the only nations blessed by God. We must stop those who want to turn our country toward the dark world, instead of toward God. We turned to God in the beginning, and we must remain a nation whose God is the Lord.

In an earlier book, I mentioned the 88/12 study by an independent unbiased institution. In that study they found that the mainstream television media, along with their cable news networks, were found to favor the Democratic Party in their reports 88 percent of the time. They favored the Republican Party only 12 percent of the time. Fox was more fair. They favored the Republican Party 60 percent of the time and the Democratic Party 40 percent of the time. Something is wrong with the three major mainstream networks, as they all come up with exactly the same percentage. In case you did not know about that study, which was done some years ago, you now know why President Trump refers to them as the "fake news" networks. If you recall, President Obama said that Fox was not a legitimate news network. Since it has been a while since the 88/12 study was done, I began a study for myself. Along with others, I intentionally watch one of the three mainstream news reports just about every day. Immediately after watching them, I switched to the Christian Broadcasting Network (CBN) and found that there was a vast difference. As a result of this new study, there is one thing I can report for sure. It is my personal opinion based on observations that there is good reason to believe that our mainstream networks are under the influence of Satan by not reporting the full truth. God does not lie. Misleading the truth is also a form of lying. If a news agency reports only what they want you to know they are misleading the viewers. That is the same as lying. Jesus said that Satan was the father of lies and that he has been a murderer and liar from the beginning.

As the mainstream folks state quite often, what they report is the truth, but they certainly are *not* reporting the whole truth. They choose to report only the things they want you to hear just as Satan does in his evil trickery. One can only conclude that they do not report things they do not want you to hear. There is much more that is reported on CBN which you do not hear on the mainstream networks. In particular, the truth about what President Trump and the Republican Party have been successful in getting accomplished.

For example, the mainstream guys fail to report what Dr. Ben Carson, Dr. Martin Luther King Jr.'s niece, and other people of color have to say. They state that President Trump is not a racist, *yet the fake news networks frequently infer by broadcasting the interviews of those who have bad things to say about our president. Specifically, that he is a racist. Again, they do this by only interviewing those who claim his being a racist to be the truth.* They know very well that it is not the whole truth. The people of color I mentioned speak favorably of President Trump and the Republican Party platform when it comes to looking out for our citizens of color. Hundreds of thousands more jobs have been created for the people of color than ever before under the Trump administration. There is a case in which they intentionally lied, not just failing to report all the truth but outright lied. I will disclose this later. You, as an American citizen, just might want to watch CBN or Fox to find out the real truth. I no longer have cable, so I cannot report what Fox news is reporting currently. However, when I did have cable, I found they reported both sides of any debate and left it up to the audience to make up their own decision as to what is the truth.

Even the companies like Facebook, Twitter, and Instagram are right now being investigated as to why many Christian-based entries are banned as if censored. A government agency like the FCC needs to step in and assure that the truth is told. I do not understand why the FCC does not hold the mainstream media accountable for the obvious failure to tell all the truth. That is, the whole truth without censorship.

I received one message from God concerning Hollywood, California. If you remember, I said earlier that California is the place which the Cherokee call, "The place where the crazy people live." I also mentioned earlier that Satan has infiltrated and/or influenced the leaders of our schools and colleges and those in the movie and television industries, as well as our government offices. There is much financial support from the rich in Hollywood for those in government offices which are held by the so-called Progressive

Democrats who openly advocate socialism. They would love to see more Progressive Democrats take over additional offices in order to give them the majority and full control of all three branches of our government. I wonder if those in the industries just mentioned know what socialism means and what will become of our country.

If they take over the White House, Senate, and House of Representatives, I believe our country is doomed to become a third world country and will be headed by a dictatorship with all of our rights under our current Constitution thrown out the window. I say this not from my own mind, but this is part of what God told me about what will happen if we do not succeed in changing our culture's path. These are the same people who want to convert our nation into a socialist nation. Please remember that socialism and communism is the same thing but just under a different name. Do we want to be like Cuba, the old Soviet Union, North Korea, Iran, and Communist China?

Now the question is, will God intervene with his own actions rather than rely only on his words being written by the many new prophets he has created in order to see that his will shall be done? Even though God's will and predictions are written by these new prophets, will the people listen and take head and obey God's wishes as he expresses in his inspired words?

Do not think that Christian ethics and beliefs are the fought only by the Progressive Democrats or the Democratic Party in general. There are other parts of our government which we are now seeing a move to "surrender to an atheist campaign against religious freedom in the military." This is evident by the actions of the Department of Defense (DoD). Here are five things that are going on right now.

That after meeting with the atheist pressure group "Military Religious Freedom Foundations," civilian DoD bureaucrats made it a crime for chaplains and soldiers to share their Christian faith, punishable by court-martial and possible imprisonment.

That in 2011 the Walter Reed National Military Medical Center banned Bible reading at its service hospital (until pressure to reverse the policy).

That the Air Force Academy, under atheist pressure, removed the words "So help me God" from the sacred oath sworn by academy recruits.

That a DoD training directive put Christians in the same category as the Islamist terror group that attacked the US on September 11, 2001.

That US military commanders have been prohibited from informing their units about programs and services offered by chaplains.

In addition to these evil acts, there is a new report as of Sunday, November 10, 2019, that witchcraft arts are being used to cast an evil spell on President Trump. This is becoming very widespread and simply adds to the evil influence Satan is casting on the earth. This is why God is now pouring out his Spirit upon the earth in the form of many new prophets like me in order to counter this attack by Satan. Remember what the scriptures say in the book of Revelation.

> He said to me: (*Jesus said to John while in heaven in the spirit*) It is done. I am the Alpha and the Omega, the Beginning And the End. To the thirsty I will give water without cost from the spring of the water of life. Those who are victorious will inherit all this, and I will be their God and they will be my children. But the cowardly, the unbelieving, the vile, the murderers, the sexually immoral, those who practice magic arts, the idolaters and all liars—they will be consigned to the fiery lake of burning sulfur. This is the second death. (Revelation 21:6–8)

> Jesus said, "Look, I am coming soon! My reward is with me, and I will give to each person according to what they have done. I am the Alpha and the Omega, the First and the Last, the Beginning and the End. Blessed are those who wash their robes, that they may have the right to the tree of

life and may go through the gates into the city.
Outside are the dogs, those who practice magic
arts, the sexually immoral, the murderers, the
idolaters and everyone who loves the practices
falsehood. I, Jesus, have sent my angel to give
you this testimony for the churches. I am the
Root and the Offspring of David, and the bright
Morning Star." (Revelation 22:12–16)

To those who say that I, the author and one of many new prophets, interject some of my own feelings into this book; that I am not able to keep from doing so because it comes from my subconscious are listening to Satan and his demons. God would not tell anyone to state such an evil thing. The words I use match the scriptures I quote. Therefore, the words I use are those God tells me to write so that the people who read this book know what God wants them to know. What I write is definitely not the things Satan wants you to know. Use common sense so that you will know the truth. What God says and what God tells me to say as a prophet is the truth. I do not state those things Satan wants you to know. He and his demons do that, as well as those they recruit who they know will fall easily for their trickery. It is well-known to preachers that Satan studies each human creation of God to find their weaknesses and their desires. He then makes those desires readily available by telling those without wisdom and knowledge that it is not a bad thing to do. It is just like he told Eve in the Garden of Eden those lies for which she fell.

I don't know how you feel about these actions, but I personally see them as severely aggressive anti-God actions and policies. So when I say I do not know how a true Christian can be actively supporting the Democratic Party and agreeing with the similar actions by the DoD, they are supporting policies and platforms that are completely anti-God. The quotes from Revelation states that those who practice the evil things listed will not enter heaven, for "they will be consigned to the fiery lake of burning sulfur." Those are Jesus's own words, not from my subconscious.

I now wish to report some disturbing news I received in the form of telepathic messages from God, but I am giving it time before including these bits of information in this book. If you read my book about knowing if a message is from God or from Satan pretending to be God, you should not jump too quick to take action. I stated that because Satan is an impatient entity. We should wait for ample signs or messages to come before deliberating over who sent them. The information I am receiving include the destruction of cities. I will say no more until I know for sure it was from God and not Satan pretending to be God.

The reason I am being hesitant is I do not know if that means cities of evil countries or cities within our own borders. Until I can determine which is the case, I will not tell everything I am currently receiving. I also wrote previously that if messages are of good things, it is probably from God. If you receive messages about bad things, it may be Satan. Therefore, it is written that we are to not act too quickly. Give Satan time to see if he becomes impatient and divulges that the messages are from him rather than from God. Today I received information about earthquakes and possible tsunamis. If both are true, then we need to know where this will happen, unless God does not yet want the people to know which cities are to be destroyed. That is only one possible explanation as to why I am not receiving all of the facts yet.

The total destruction of certain cities is not something I want to pass on to the people unless God tells me to do so. As yet he has not told me if it is cities in evil countries or cities in our own country. This may be depending on if our own country is considered to be evil by God. Our God Almighty is in charge, and whatever he wants to happen will happen. Therefore, until I know the whole truth about this subject, I will say nothing more. In fact, the subject of the destruction of complete cities is something bad, but God has been known to destroy complete cities in the Old Testament along with surrounding cities. Remember what God did with Sodom and Gomorrah because of their evilness. God hates evilness.

If God assures me and/or other prophets, what will happen is based on his desires. I only know for sure that God wants evilness to be destroyed and righteousness prevail.

Many members of the Democratic Party even brag about becoming a socialist nation. At one point, the *New York Times* reported in big letters, "We Are All Socialists Now." Don't the stockholders and leaders of the *New York Times* along will all other media realize that they will be out of a job? A socialist nation must control all news reporting so that the people only read, see, and hear what they want them to. In the old Soviet Union, the state news media was called *Pravda.* There will be only one newspaper and one television network. It will be state owned and operated just like in North Korea, China, Cuba, and other dictatorships or socialist nations.

Some, like Bernie Sanders, even classifies himself as a socialist but runs under the Democratic Party platform as well as the foursome known as the squad. The ACLU is another Democratic Party spinoff of sorts. The ACLU fights anything that resembles a threat to the socialists' agenda and their ultimate goal. If you remember, it was the southern Democrats that founded the KKK and made all the laws of segregation. They do not care about the people. They care about themselves. I mentioned earlier about the book by George Orwell *Animal Farm.* It tells how the pigs on the farm who represent communists take over the farm, and all the other animals are worse off than they were when under the ownership of the cruel farmer they murdered.

There was a time not too many decades ago when a socialist could not get elected to the office of dog catcher. Now they are welcomed by many who live in the dark world headed by Satan. Those who commit the terrible crimes mentioned previously are the same people who will run our lives. In the end, they will be casted into the fire along with Satan. The way things are going that time may not be too far off.

God has instructed me to quote again the scripture John 15:18–25, where Jesus states,

> If the world hates you, keep in mind that it hated me first. If you belonged to the world, it would love you as its own. As it is, you do not belong to the world, but I have chosen you out of the world. That is why the world hates you. Remember what

I told you: "A servant is not greater than his master." If they persecuted me they will persecute you also. If they obeyed my teaching, they will obey yours also. They will treat you this way because of my name, for they do not know the one who sent me. If I had not come and spoken to them, they would not be guilty of sin; but ow they have no excuse for their sin. Whoever hates me hates my father as well. If I had not done among them the works no one else did, they would not be guilty of sin. As it is, they have seen, and yet they have hated both me and my Father. But this is to fulfill what is written in their Law: "They hated me without reason."

It is obvious to many in this country that the socialists belong to the world. According to the Bible and Jesus's teaching, the dark world is under the ownership and control of Satan. When your judgment day arrives, would you rather be able to enter heaven, or would you rather spend eternity with the evil one in the lake of fire?

God wants you to remember his inspired words in John 35, "You will have the light just a little while longer. Walk in the light while you have the light, before darkness overtakes you. Whoever walks in the dark does not know where they are going. Believe in the light while you have the light, so that you may become children of light."

Only those who believe in God and his only Son, Jesus, have the power to stop the darkness overtaking us. We vote for those who would have our country continue to be blessed by God. Because of the wealth of those who contribute to the politicians that favor socialism, voting by those who oppose socialism must assume the duty of voting in great numbers.

God wanted me to quote the prophet Isaiah who wrote in chapter 42:1–11 something that pertains to what is happening yet today.

"Here is my servant, whom I uphold, my chosen one in whom I delight; I will put my Spirit on him, and he will bring justice to the nations. He will not shout or cry out, or raise his voice in the streets. A bruised reed he will not break, and a smoldering wick he will not snuff out. In faithfulness he will bring forth justice; he will not falter or be discouraged till he establishes justice on earth. In his teaching the islands will put their hope.

This is what God the Lord says—the Creator of the heavens, who stretches them out, who spreads out the earth with all that springs from it, who gives breath to its people, and life to those who walk on it: "I, the Lord, have called you in righteousness; I will take hold of your hand. I will keep you and will take you to be a covenant for the people and a light for the Gentiles, to open eyes that are blind, to free captives from prison and to release from the dungeon those who sit in darkness.

I am the Lord; that is my name! I will not yield my glory to another or my praise to idols. See, the former things have taken place and new things I declare; before they spring into being I announce them to you."

The quoting of that last passage has sparked a thought that God does want me to pass on to the people. God said that he may withhold passing down to the people what his plan is. He said, "Before they spring not being I announce them to you." That means to me that God has a total plan, but certain parts will not be announced through his prophets until the timing is right.

Today, Saturday, October 19, 2019, I received a message that contains either of two options God has in store: (1) He may decide to cause cities to be destroyed and unusual weather conditions destroy crops, which will cause an economic nightmare for our country. (2) He may also do the same in any and/or all countries that have decided to turn away from him. That means that we must try our best to keep those who would lead us down a path of ultimate destruction by God from becoming our leaders in this country. When God wants to announce his plans to the people, he will tell the prophets what to say. At this point, he is not telling me what his plan is, but he is at least telling me what options he has before him. He already knows which options he plans to take but does not yet want to divulge those plans to the people just yet.

Now for the issue of the mainstream media actually lying, it concerns the group of four congresswomen known as the squad. I would like to remind every reader what God told Abram before he changed his name to Abraham in Genesis 12: "The Lord had said to Abram, Go from your country, your people and your father's household to the land I will sow you. I will make you into a great nation, and I will bless you; I will make your name great, and you will be a blessing. I will bless those who bless you, and whoever curses you I will curse; and all peoples on earth will be blessed through you" (Geneses 12:1–3).

God is speaking of the creation of Israel. The squad was asked to not attend a meeting of members of the House of Representatives in Israel recently. They have been very outspoken and cursing Israel. God said he will curse those people. God cannot lie. Therefore, do not join in with those who do what God demands us not to do. Otherwise you will have to pay dearly. Now try to remember what you heard on the mainstream media. They not only withheld the whole truth; they knowingly lied. They reported that President Trump picked on the members of the squad because they were women of color. People around the world knew, as well as the state of Israel and all news media, that President Trump picked on the squad's anti-Semitic comments and not because of their color or being women. They also failed to report the words of those people of color who know President Trump and know he is not a racist. In my opinion, they are *making the news rather than reporting the news*. That should be illegal. If you want to know the truth about what is happening in the world, turn off the mainstream media and tune into CBN News Channel, the CBN channel, or Fox News.

President Trump is often accused by the mainstream media for causing violence. What about the things the squad said? Shortly after their anti-Semitic comments, we have a man going into a synagogue and killing as many Jews as he can. Is there a pattern here? That is for you to determine based on the real truth. I am not making this up. I am reporting what I saw and heard on the mainstream media.

The mainstream media is not the only cause of the collapse of your culture if we fail to succeed. The overall Christian Church is to share the blame. From the beginning of Christianity, it was the job of the church to teach the people so that their evolving culture would not drift toward the dark world of Satan and away from God. Yes, we attend serviced to worship our Lord, but we also attend church to learn everything Christians can be taught straight from the Bible. Somehow, this has changed. Many denominations have allowed the culture to influence the teachings of the church. Christians look to the Christian church leaders as biblical experts who should know that Satan is behind the infiltration of our culture with his trickery. All churches should have stood firm and teach what God has instructing us to do and to learn all that is to be learned from his inspired words in the Holy Bible. Some churches did do right, but others are guilty of not being brave enough to teach all of the truth and fight Satan.

Satan's trickery has caused many good Christian to fall just as if they were the angels that fell out of heaven with the evil one. Many churches have given in to his trickery, and all of our society must pay the price for their mistake.

Those churches and those pastors of churches who teach directly from the Bible are more like the early churches. When the early churches began to sway in the wrong direction, away from God, it was the apostles who wrote letters of correction that kept them on the right course. That is why those letters to the early churches should still be our guide today. It is not. When churches mislead its members by not teaching everything those letters were intended to teach, they have allowed themselves to be influenced by Satan's trickery. The people went to church to worship our Father in heaven. Instead, they unknowingly were guided in the wrong direction.

Only those churches and pastors who teach directly from the Bible tell it like it is. They pass on to their congregation the truth that God has written within his inspiration words without fear of hurting someone's feelings because they do not believe what God tells them.

In 2 Timothy 3:1–5 are the inspired words of God concerning what will happen in the last days. God has instructed me to be tell what will happen in the future if we fail to succeed to guide people in the right direction, guide them to stay aiming for God and not the dark world of Satan. Instead of thinking this quote as simply words of Paul writing to Timothy, we must remember that they *are the inspired words of God who told Paul to write these words.* Here is the entire quote of 2 Timothy 3:1–5: "But mark this: There will be terrible times in the last days. People will be lovers of themselves, lovers of money, boastful, proud, abusive, disobedient to their parents, ungrateful, unholy, without love, unforgiving, slanderous, without self-control, brutal, not lovers of the good, treacherous, rash, conceited, lovers of pleasure rather than lovers of God—having a form of godliness but denying its power. Have nothing to do with such people."

If we fail to succeed, God tells us through Paul in this second letter to his good friend Timothy, who became the first deacon of the Christian Church, what will happen if we fail to stay with God, stay in the light rather than be swayed toward the dark world. Yes, the Church itself is partly to blame for our possible demise. They failed to stick to the teachings of God in favor of appeasing those who are the leaders in our dark culture which has been overtaken by Satan.

Please remember what Jesus said in John 12:35–36. "You are going to have the light just a little while longer. Walk in the light while you have the light, before darkness overtakes you. Whoever walks in the dark does not know where they are going. Believe in the light while you have the light, so that you may become children of light."

Please, my fellow Christians, join the fight against the darkness overtaking our culture. Find out what God wants you, as an individual, to do for him in his battle with Satan. For God has given each of us something to do for him. Find out what job God had in store for you from the time even before you were in your mother's womb. Stand up boldly against those who would murder babies even at the time of their birth. Those who commit such a horrible deed must answer to God for killing something he created and even had a plan for what that baby would become once it grows up to be an adult. Also, help by walking in the light while you still have the light. Don't just think because you were born again that there is nothing else you need to do. You must strive to be more fruitful. If you don't, you are liable to be tossed away to wither. Then you could be thrown into the fire with all the others who were wither not born again or used their free will to turn away from God, the Creator of everything. One can only enter heaven through Jesus. Jesus said, "Nobody will enter the kingdom of God except through me."

There is an event taking place in our government even as this book is being written. It is the appearance of a so-called whistleblower who somehow has spoken but has yet to be seen.

Being a former computer software developer and problem solver for many decades, I am somewhat an expert in the use of pure logic. God has not told me what the outcome of this whistleblower's accusations will be. However, it has just been announced that the whistleblower will not testify. The Democrats say they no longer need him, because the information given to them by President Trump about the phone call is all they need.

The Democrats under the direction of House Speaker Nancy Pelosi have been trying very hard to find something they can use to begin an impeachment proceeding against our sitting president. They wanted to find something, anything that will be grounds for impeachment. They have had a hard time coming up with anything substantial. Then out of nowhere, a whistleblower appears, but his identity must be kept secret. Why? I have no idea. If what he knows is the truth, then there is no reason to hide him from the citizens.

Meanwhile, the president states that he believes Hunter Biden, Joe Biden's son, is guilty of illegal activities involving his work with the government of Ukraine. If what the president suspects is true, then there should be an investigation done by the president of Ukraine. If this illegal activity is possibly also involving Hunter Biden in the country of Australia, then the president of Australia should also be involved in any such investigation in order to expose the truth. Since the illegal activities possibly involve the governments of Ukraine and Australia, then the presidents of these two countries should know about any wrongdoing that may be taking place in their countries. They *should be asked to assist* in finding out the truth. Finding the truth has nothing to do with trying to discredit Joe Biden from being nominated to run against President Trump in the 2020 election. It has everything to do with exposing possible illegal activities by Joe Biden's son.

The logical thing to do is to ask, "Who stands to gain by the appearance of this whistleblower?" It is those who want to impeach President Trump—the Democratic Party. Somehow, they magically found possible grounds for impeachment to which they can at least investigate. If it turns out to be a false witness, then they have lost nothing and do not come away looking like a bunch of idiots just trying to find false and unfounded grounds for impeachment. If the whistleblower is kept secret and lies under the direction of Satan, who Jesus said is the father of lies, then they have found grounds for impeachment even if they are false.

As a true Christian, I do believe that God already knows the outcome of the 2020 election. He is not going to tell me or any other prophet, because that would not be the right thing to do, and God does not lie, nor does he do anything that would not be the right thing to do. My greatest concern right now is that the Democrats are doing everything they can come up with to follow through with impeachment proceedings and make President Trump look bad before the 2020 election. I believe they will stop at nothing to try to win the election and get their anti-God platform in place, and they will have succeeded in causing the United States of America to be no longer blessed by God. They have nothing to lose but everything to gain. This all makes perfectly logical sense.

Now I wish to give you what God did tell me what will happen if we do not succeed in turning our culture around and aim it in the same direction our founding fathers intended. That is one nation under God with a platform that does not include any influence by

Satan and his demons. While some of the things I now pass on to you, the readers of this book, it also includes everything God told me what will happen to our wonderful country if we do not succeed in turning our culture back to God's direction and stay away from the dark world of Satan.

We will become a socialist or communist nation. Just like the old United Soviet Socialist Republic (USSR), we will be the new USSR, the United States Socialist Republic. The Constitution will be thrown away, and all that our founding fathers built will be destroyed. That means we will no longer have the freedom of speech, freedom of religion, or freedom to bear arms. The actions by the DoD as reported earlier leaves no doubt that this is their goal.

In a communist nation, the leader or dictator is considered god, and we will no longer be allowed to worship the Creator, our heavenly Father, the Father of his one and only Son, Jesus. To worship our God is to say that the dictator is not god. Therefore, just like in China and North Korea and other countries today, Christians will be persecuted, churches will be burned, pastors will be murdered or put in prison, and all Bibles will be burned. Homes will be searched for any Christian material, and if found, the residents will be punished or murdered, and their Christian materials will be destroyed. Everyone will be ordered to spy on their family members and neighbors and report any violations in practicing those things which are no longer allowed by law. No praying in private or public.

There will be no unions to protect worker rights. Workers will have no rights. Pay and very few benefits will be dictated by the government. The government will be the employer of every citizen. You will be given a job which the government decides, and you have no say so in what you will do for a living.

There will be famine. Very little food will be available, because the government will spend most of its money on building the military. Just like in the old Soviet Union, people will wait in long lines to get one loaf of bread which must last the week. Very little meat will be available. If you want, you can grow potatoes and other veggies in a small home garden. However, many will live in government housing which is actually small apartments. Like in the Soviet Union, there may be as many as seven families in one small apartment. Infrastructure will gradually decay due to no funding for repair. We will become a third world country like we are used to seeing in Africa and other extremely poor nations.

If this is the kind of country you wish to live in, then join those who advocate socialism in our Senate and House of Representatives. They lie about what they promise knowing that those who obtain high positions in the new communist party will be the ones who earn lots of money. There will be no rich from which they can tax heavily. There will be no commercials to advertise competitive products. All products will be manufactured by the government. Now you know why those who want this kind of government do not say where the money will come from to provide free college for all and free medical care for all. You will get the kind of medical care that was available in the old Soviet Union. Plus, like the governments of China and North Korea, the people will suffer greatly in order to spend any money the government has on missiles, weapons of war, and millions of military personnel.

I would now like to leave you with several thoughts. I ask that you remember what Jesus said to those who were about to stone a prostitute. He said, "Whoever is without sin let him cast the first stone." Everyone walked away because none of us is perfect; none of us is without sin. Only Jesus is perfect. Therefore, just because our president makes mistakes, please do not be too harsh on him and decide to be in favor of impeachment or voting for someone who has done less for our country. President Trump is not perfect. Let he or she who is perfect cast the first stone by their vote to get rid of our president. If you think you are perfect and have never made a mistake, never say something that you later regret saying nor made a wrong decision, then you have every right to try to get President Trump out of office. Many other presidents have done much worse things in years past. Mistakes by a president are nothing new. Presidents are human.

"Give thanks to the Lord for he is good. His mercy endures forever" (Psalm 106:1).

I now pray for all who live in this country of freedom. Father God, I ask that you continue to bless the United States and its people. May its people strive to learn the truth and not the lies of Satan, who is the father of lies since the beginning. I ask this in Jesus's name, amen.

CHAPTER 12

As the ninth chapter was being written, I was told by God that I was considered a prophet. But one thing was missing. I had yet to receive any insight into the future. Then completing chapter 10, I was given a look into the future. The message from God tells more about what may happen if we are not able to turn our culture around back to God and turn it away from the dark world of Satan. At the time this eleventh chapter was inspired, God also wanted a quote to be added as a warning.

> A nation is not conquered from without until it
> has destroyed itself from within. (W. Durant)

The words written in the eleventh chapter were sent in a message from God, but it contained much more detail than what was told in chapter 11. I decided to go ahead and submit the book upon completion, which ended with chapter 11 in late 2019 because the Christian book market was already flooded because of God's pouring out his Holy Spirit upon the earth to battle the pouring out of Satan's spirit.

Chapter 11 ends without the entire message from God included. The entire message tells of some things about the future that seem extremely disturbing to me and probably to readers as well. Doing what the Bible teaches, I wanted to make sure the message I was hearing was actually from God and not from Satan pretending to be God. Knowing there was time to wait because of the hold placed on the publication of new Christian books, I intentionally put the rest of the disturbing message to the test as stated in the Bible. The Bible says not to rush into action when we hear something that may be from Satan pretending to be God. Yes, Satan loves to do that.

So I decided to use the wait time to see if Satan would show his true colors and become upset that his message was not included in the book. Upon the book being sent to the editing department, I decided to include the rest of the message in the book. I wish to explain that God assured me that what I am about to say was from him. Also, I wish to emphasize the fact that God said these things may, I repeat, may happen if we fail to turn our culture around to God and away from Satan's dark world. Jesus said that those who live in the dark world do not know where they are going. Now when you read this, the newly added twelfth chapter, you will read the rest of the message that was sent from God.

Because of the nature of the message that God instructed to be written, I want to remind all readers one important fact. God has often used bad things and turned them around to become good things. He does this quite often. Those who know and understands his ways know that he does turn bad things into good, even our daily lives. Sometimes, he even does it on a more widespread basis. That is he may do this with one area, one nation, or even the worldwide.

Please do not become angry with God for things you do not understand or of which you fail to approve. Please remember that he is the boss. Just like the rules parents set down to their children and then rebuke them when they do wrong by breaking those rules, God does the same thing. Both our earthly parents and God loves his children. As you probably know, he does rebuke his children like earthly parents because he loves them and wants to protect them from harm or danger. What God included in his message to me may be hard to understand and even cause a person to wonder what is going on. In various places in the Bible, God's inspired words warn us against hardening our hearts against him. It states that one could end up a God-hater. This does not please God at all. Even when a person's child at any age passes, they must not blame God. He is in control.

God said if we do not change our culture's direction, there are several things that will happen. They are the following:

1. There will be disease. Yes, this part did already happen. I am speaking of COVID-19. God wants you to now that he knew it would happen. It makes no difference if it was caused by animal sales in China, the Hunan laboratory making a mistake, it was done by man intentionally, or even if God himself set the disease upon us. God is all-knowing. He knows everything that will come to pass in the future regardless of its source.

2. There will be famine. Many will starve throughout the world. It may strike harder in those places where the culture is so far into the dark world there is no possibility of a change in direction. Those are the countries where its leader is god and churches and Bibles are burned. Even the preachers are often tortured and/or killed.

3. God also mentioned in his message that some cities will be destroyed. God did not go into detail as to the cause of the destruction. It could be by a natural disaster or it may be due to the decline in the economy worldwide as a result of COVID-19. There are three cities in the United States that are targeted for probable destruction. I was given a vision of the United States, and I was told by way of that vision where some cities are. There may be three or four or more. I will not disclose the names of the cities because God does not want me to cause a sudden panic. That would serve no purpose. For any city that now recognizes it has been heading in the wrong direction, it would be wise to make sure you change the ways of your cities' culture.

4. He wants everyone to remember what he told Abram, which is written in Genesis 12.

I will make you a great nation (Israel) and I will bless those who bless you (Israel) and I will curse those who curse you (Israel). If the culture in

your city is guilty of these thing it is advisable for
you to change your culture.

5. God knew the COVID-19 virus would strike many people
    in the world. How do I know he knew? Because it was
    mentioned in the message he gave me. When chapters 10
    through 11 of this book was submitted for publication, I
    knew about the disease and famine and the destruction of
    some cities because of the message given to me.

Now you know why I hesitated to include these things in the
eleventh chapter. I wanted to make sure that it was truly God who
told me these things and not Satan.

If you have been observing the people during this pandemic,
you will see some good already begging to happen. People of all walks
of life are donating food and supplies, helping to serve in food dis-
tribution centers, people who are stuck in their homes are making
masks and face shields for those in the hospitals and clinics. These
things show we are a caring people, and we know we are all in this
together. People are even tuning into and listening to God for direction as to what they can do to help. Prayers are conducted openly in
public. These are exactly the things the Democratic party platform
and atheists are trying to eliminate. Thank God for the pouring out
of his Spirit upon the people so that some good can come out of
COVID-19.

Please remember three things about heaven:

1. While I mention God often in this and other books, you
    must keep in mind that upon Jesus rising from the dead
    after being tortured and crucified, the Father gave Jesus
    complete dominion over the entire universe—all God's
    creation. He is actually sitting in his Father's throne with
    him.
2. The Bible tells us that when we have troubles, God will
    always provide a way out. We need to look for it. It may
    not be easy to spot if you live in the dark world or if you do

not have a strong enough faith. Believe in what God tells you. If you need a way out, pray with all sincerity for him to please show you the way out that he said he will provide.

3. God will hear the prayers of those who pray for help and guidance during troubling times. If you realize you have been heading in the wrong direction and away from God, please repent. Tell God you are sorry and ask for his forgiveness. If you are serious and sincere in your prayer, he will forgive you and welcome you back as one of his children—children of light. During these times of COVID-19, it is important for you to let your wondrous light shine so that you can feel good that you helped others who are suffering. This is certainly a time for us to think about the phrase, "Let there be light."

May God bless you and be gracious unto you and give you peace today and forever more.

The End

ABOUT THE AUTHOR

Much of the history behind the author has been told in the first book God inspired him to write. That was because God wanted to explain how he has a plan for each of us. In the case of the author, God's plan was for him to ultimately become one of many new prophets. That is to tell all people what God wants them to know by reading his, God's, books. God is the true author.

The human author wants to stress that he is of little importance except being a servant of God. He simply writes the books that God directs him to write. You may choose to disbelieve what the author has written, but keep in mind that what he writes is what God and his Son, Jesus, told him to write. Therefore, you are either disbelieving God and Jesus or disbelieving the fact that God and Jesus inspired him in writing of this book. Almost everything that is written in this book is backed up by scriptures. Therefore, the words of the Bible are God's inspired words, as well as the books and other writings by his prophets. It has always been that way.

The author wants you to remember one thing. Everything you see, hear, and touch was created by God's words. His words hold all the power in the universe, including everything in heaven and on earth. So when God has a human to write his words down so everyone can read, then you are reading the Words of God and not simply the words of a human.

It may seem strange to the average person, but God does direct prophets and others to write down what he wants people to know. This is done while the author is living in the Spirit. This book explains about how living in the Spirit works. As a preview here is how that works. It is as though God and his Son, Jesus, enters the room where the author is to do his writing. Then it is as though they place a sign on the door outside "Do Not Disturb." The author is then in constant communications with the Father and his Son. They tell him what is going to be written. The author begins to research the Bible to make sure that everything written is backed up by scriptures. He then begins to write while God and Jesus look on. They often interrupt the author to tell him or her to backspace a few words or an entire sentence and put in the words they want to be written. Yes, the book is written down to the exact wording God wishes to use.

In case you have not heard on the news, scientists have discovered a part of the human brain that they call the God particle. Even when a person is in a coma or unconscienced, there is a part of the brain that appears to be communicating to an entity somewhere in the universe. The communications seems to be going in both directions. Christians already know that the Holy Spirit in those who are born again will help guide the individual. Here is an example. If someone tells a righteous person to go into a store and steal something, the person gets a guilty feeling. That is the Holy Spirit telling the person that it is wrong to do this. Do not obey the person telling you to do something that is wrong and against God's teaching in the Bible.

CPSIA information can be obtained
at www.ICGtesting.com
Printed in the USA
FSHW011703021220
76391FS